MENTAL DISORDERS
& SPIRITUAL HEALING

*Teachings from
the Early Christian East*

Jean-Claude Larchet

MENTAL DISORDERS
&
SPIRITUAL HEALING

*Teachings from
the Early Christian East*

Translated by
Rama P. Coomaraswamy
G. John Champoux

ANGELICO PRESS
SOPHIA PERENNIS

Originally published in French as
Thérapeutique des maladies mentales
© Les Éditions du Cerf, 1992
English translation © Sophia Perennis 2005
First English Edition 2005
Angelico Press / Sophia Perennis edition 2011
All rights reserved

Series editor: James R. Wetmore

For information, address:
Angelico Press / Sophia Perennis, P.O. Box 151011
San Rafael, CA 94915
angelicopress.com
sophiaperennis.com

Library of Congress Cataloging-in-Publication Data

Larchet, Jean-Claude, 1949–
[Thérapeutique des maladies mentales. English]
Mental disorders and spiritual healing:
teachings from the early Christian east /
Jean-Claude Larchet; translated by G. John Champoux,
Rama P. Coomaraswamy.—1st English ed.

p. cm.

Includes bibliographical references and index.
ISBN 1 59731 045 X (pbk: alk. paper)
ISBN 1 59731 061 1 (hardcover: alk. paper)
1. Mental illness—Religious aspects—Orthodox Eastern Church.
2. Psychotherapy—Religious aspects—Orthodox Eastern Church.
3. Spiritual healing—History of doctrines—Early church, ca. 30–600.
4. Psychiatry and religion. I. Title.
RC 455. 4. R4L3713 2005

616.89'14—dc22   2005015423

CONTENTS

INTRODUCTION

REGARDLESS OF HISTORICAL PERIOD or the nature of the society involved, mental illness has been always with us. And even within any given society one often finds contradictory attitudes taken towards the insane. Some view these unfortunates as messengers from above, as mediators between man and God, and hence worthy of respect and veneration, even elevating them to the function of priest or the dignity of prophet; others consider them less than human, as the associates or slaves of evil powers, as individuals to be persecuted, avoided, and even imprisoned or physically eliminated.

At the same time, the nature and cause of what we like to call 'mental illness' have always posed tremendous difficulties. They raise many issues with regard to their causes, their manifestations and their origins, and these in relation to the three dimensions of the human being—physical, psychic and spiritual—and all this in a much more pressing manner than with those illnesses primarily affecting the body.

It is rare that all three dimensions are taken into consideration by those who have attempted to explain these problems, and, in examining the history of psychiatry (as usually understood), even those doing so have had great difficulty in integrating all three and usually end up splitting them apart while favoring one or the other.[1]

Paradoxically modern psychiatry is afflicted with many internal conflicts that result in theories and therapies that are heterogeneous and even at times contradictory. The classical study *Manuel de psychiatrie* by H. Ey, P. Pernard, and C. Brisset delineates four basic theoretical positions: (1) organo-mechanistic theories which consider that mental illness has an organic origin; (2) psychodynamic

1. See H. Ey. 'Histoire de la psychiatrie' *Encyclopédie médico-chirugicale*, 1955, 37005A; *Études psychiatriques*, I, Paris, 1952. Y. Pélicier, *Histoire de la psychiatrie*, Paris, 1971, F. G. Alexander et S. Selesnick *Histoire de la psychiatrie*, Paris, 1972.

theories based on unconscious pathology which hold that these illness are the result of unconscious forces (Freud and his disciples;
Jung); (3) socio-psychogenic theories that consider environmental
factors of primary importance and which see mental illness as a
pathological psychological reaction to unfortunate situations or difficulties (the Anglo-Saxon school; Pavlov) or as the effect of trau-
mas of communication, especially within the bosom of the family
(Bateson, Watzlawick and the Palo Alto school); (4) organogenic
dynamic theories which hold that mental illnesses are the result of
the breakdown of the psychic being which is affected by organic factors (Jackson, Janet, Ey).

These different outlooks are in principle mutually exclusive: the
first advocates a purely organic etiology and totally rejects psychological and sociological factors; the second considers psychological
factors as primary and denies any fundamental role to organic factors, though it admits the importance of certain related factors
which are held to be endogenous; the third rejects all organic etiologies and denies any role to the unconscious. Mental illness is seen as
purely the result of exogenous factors. The fourth excludes all such
factors including the role of the unconscious. It attributes mental
illness to an organic substratum but it denies any direct or mechan-
ical relationship between this substratum and symptoms. It does
however recognize that dynamic psychic forces play an essential role
in the evolution of mental illnesses.[1]

Even within any given position one frequently finds considerable
variation in theory and practice, to say nothing of divergences and
even contradictions. (This is particularly true when one considers
the various psychotherapies such as Freudian or Jungian psychoanalysis.)

In the practical order it is clear that many psychiatrists are in
practice eclectic. Unable to show that there is any coherent manner
of understanding these illnesses, it is only to be expected that such
should be the case.

---

1. Cf. H. Ey, P. Bernard, C. Brisset, *Manuel de psychiatrie*, Paris, 1974 (4th ed.),
pp 68–76.

All the different approaches to therapy claim success.[1] The fact that such heterogeneous therapies, founded as they are on a different and even contradictory theories, can have similar results violates the logical principle of non-contradiction and leads one to think that efficacy is the result of something other than their specificity, such as the attention or direction given to the patient, and such as might well occur outside of a professional milieu.

Looking at things from a negative point of view, one could also conclude that the various therapies are equally ineffective, or when effective are so only because they encounter a nature that, in such situations and according to the ancient Hippocratic principle, is capable of finding ways to heal itself.

Moreover, in many cases of both neurosis and psychosis these therapies are of little help. Psychotropic medications will act to alleviate symptoms, but in most cases have no effect on underlying causes. While they unquestionably act to relieve distressing symptoms, it is often only at the cost of an internal and external inhibition and blunting of affect that causes as much distress to the patient as did the original illness. Many psychiatrists recognize the fact that these medications are only adjuvants whose greatest value is to make the patient amenable to therapies based on psychological interventions, but such therapies are seldom used, while the medicinal approach is rarely crowned with success. One knows that psychoanalysis, one of the most elaborate forms of therapy currently available, rarely cures those afflicted with psychoses, and only attains to limited success with neuroses. Moreover, Freud never thought that a complete healing was possible, and the majority of psychoanalysts modestly limit their goals to assisting their patients deal with their problems and better support their afflictions.

The variety of psychiatric theories available makes the definition and classification of mental illnesses very difficult.[2] Hence it follows

1. See the review of J.–Y. Nau, of a study published in *The Lancet*, of July 30, 1988: 'A comparative study on the treatment of mental diseases. Psychotherapy and Psychiatric drugs compared', *Le Monde*, August 5, 1988.

2. Cf. H. Ey, P. Bernard, C. Brisset, *Manuel de psychiatrie*, pp 217–218. E. Stengel, 'Classification of mental disorders', *Bull. OMS*, no. 21, 1959, pp 600–663.

that there are considerable differences both between the schools and from one country to another. Indeed, it has been asserted that there are 'no universally accepted models of classification.'[1]

The contemporary evolution of psychiatry, far from being directed towards unification or harmonization, tends rather to accentuate the divergences and to concretize the differences. Take for example 'schizophrenia'. In France this is a well demarcated entity while in the Anglo-Saxon countries it embraces a much wider series of conditions such that at times it includes almost all the psychoses. Again, consider the distinction between psychoses and neuroses—the classic distinction between these two large categories is often contested, especially by the anti-psychiatric schools. When it comes to etiology, autism provides us with an excellent example: there is hardly an area of more lively dispute than that which exists between those who hold to a psychological verses a genetic cause.[2]

Even the very idea of mental illness poses difficulties. According to the anti-psychiatric movement that developed in the sixties, the very idea of mental illness is a myth (Szasz), something invented by society (Cooper), and is in fact not in any sense an illness. Psychiatrists using the Anglo-Saxon psychoanalytic method, by stressing the importance of social and environmental factors, similarly tended to dissolve the concept of mental illness (Sullivan). Michel Foucault in his *Histoire de la folie à l'âge classique*,[3] upholds the thesis that the concept of 'mental illness' was the result of an abusive and reductive appropriation of madness by physicians when medicine came out of the dark ages, while previous to that time it was also abusively identified with irrationality and as such excluded by a socially validated and dominant mind-set.

The attitude of institutional psychiatry reflects all these contradictions and divergences. In the actual state of affairs as noted by Henri Ey and his collaborators 'one can only vacillate between those

1. H. Ey, P. Bernard, C. Brisset, *Manuel de psychiatrie*, p217.
2. See the articles of Dr Escoffier-Lambiotte, *Le Monde*, Feb. 2, Feb. 14, April 24, 1985 and of J. –Y. Nau, *Le Monde*, July 22, 1988.
3. Paris, 1972

who were more interested in the illness than the patient, and those who were more interested in the patient than the illness.'[1]

Hospitalization itself reflected this ambiguity. When Pinel removed the chains of the mentally ill in 1793 and began to treat the insane as medical patients, they were no longer seen as outcasts, but instead found themselves fettered by the law courts and asylums. On the one hand, the hospitalization and isolation of the mentally ill might be welcomed by those excluded from their families and society,[2] but on the other hand it could also be seen as a kind of imprisonment, and indeed, in the eyes of most people the specialized hospital was a prison.

The discovery of neuroleptics seems to be a means of liberation, but as many have pointed out, this is but the substitution of a chemical straitjacket for former methods of restraint. Unquestionably great progress has been made in humanizing the conditions in mental hospitals and adjusting medications on an individual basis.[3] But the overwhelming influence of organogenic attitudes and their utilization of medications often results in limiting the care of patients to only these modalities. The psychological problems of the mentally ill—seen as epiphenomena in the light of these theories and attitudes—are rarely dealt with. The patient himself rarely derives any benefit from the hospital personnel (who are often too few in numbers and not well trained, again as a result of the above mentioned influences), other than the distribution of medications and the satisfaction of their material needs. The net result of the medicalization of mental illness is that the disease rather than the patient receives treatment. Another effect is that only the medical doctor is considered competent to treat what is considered to be a physico-chemical derangement No regard is given to the patient's will and his ability to be involved in understanding and healing himself. It is partly in response to this situation that therapeutic

---

1. H. Ey, P. Bernard, C. Brisset, *Manuel de psychiatrie*, p 61.

2. See C. Brisset, 'Psychiatry and the exclusion of the mentally ill', *Le Monde*, Nov. 2, 1977, p 9.

3. See C. Koupernik, 'L'Heure des 'treatements sur mesure'', *Le Monde*, April 16, 1980, p 15.

communities were developed by anti-psychiatric critics in England (Cooper, Lang), and the movement critical of psychiatry in Italy called *Psichiatria democratica* (Basaglia). The former insists upon making the mentally ill responsible for their manner of living and involves them in making the therapeutic decisions which affect them, while the latter attempts to provide a totally unrestricted environment and to integrate them as much as possible into normal society. Unfortunately both these efforts have remained marginal.

True, apart from institutionalization, relations with the mentally ill are always difficult and problematic. They always present a disturbing element to society and their families, and above all a challenge to established values, to the dominant concepts of normality, and hence are a danger to the stability of those around them, especially those whose stability may be fragile and only maintained with great difficulty. Unquestionably the anti-psychiatry movement exaggerates when it sees the conflicts between the mentally ill and society a healthy reaction. But it is nevertheless true that the incarceration of the mentally ill is a response to the will of society, family members or groups of individuals who feel their own equilibrium and sanity threatened. The mentally ill person is clearly and beyond doubt 'the other', someone who is radically different and, as such, is the 'stranger'. It is significant that in most societies he is seen as someone who is either superhuman or subhuman (as someone deprived of the use of reason, a faculty seen as specifically human, or as someone 'deranged' subject to non-human forces and unable to exercise his free will, another specifically human characteristic), but rarely as an ordinary person.

The study which follows is a part of a trilogy devoted to the Christian conception of illness as found in the writings of the Church Fathers and the lives of the eastern saints from the first to the fourteenth century.[1] It will attempt to contribute to the history of mental illness and its treatment in a domain little studied up to now.

---

1. The first volume considered bodily illness (*Théologie de la maladie,* Ed. Du Cerf, Paris, 1991 [available in English translation as *The Theology of Illness,* (Crestwood: SVS Press, 2002]), the second considered spiritual illness (*Therapeutique des maladies spirituelles,* 4th ed., Ed. du Cerf, Paris, 2000).

In view of the many problems which current psychiatry faces, the difficulties in understanding, the proper treatment of mental illness,[1] and the manner in which society responds to those so afflicted, we shall try to offer some insight into the manner in which early Christians viewed, understood, and treated insanity, and to show the benefits, however modest, that the thought and experience of the early Christians can provide.

It goes without saying that the social and historic context was vastly different, and that it would be inappropriate to offer all their ideas as being relevant and all their therapeutic practices as models. Clearly some aspects of mediaeval medicine are no longer tenable. Many of the ideas of Hippocrates and Galen, especially those ideas that attempted to explain mental illness or apply therapies based on them have long since been discarded.

It should also be stressed that the Fathers were not overly preoccupied with this subject and dealt with it only indirectly and intermittently. The source material, with its many gaps and fragments, does not provide us with as coherent, systemic, precise, and complete a view into the subject of mental disorders as is the case with bodily and above all spiritual illness. Also, the synthesis that we have drawn from these sources is markedly incomplete. Despite this however, apart from removing certain prejudices and correcting certain misunderstandings, we feel the views of the early Fathers offer us a variety of resources and ideas for current practice.

While modern psychiatry by and large appears to be split up into various schools, each holding to contradictory theories and claiming exclusive value for their own point of view, it is interesting to see

---

1. We do not wish to attach any pejorative sense to the term. We are only following the practice of the Fathers which sometimes used the word 'illness' (see for example S. Gregory of Nazianzus, *Carm. Theol.* II, 28, PG 37, 857A) but most often the word 'folly' (*folie*). This last concept has much broader implications than the former term and provides a better insight into their pluridimentional conceptions. The first is more familiar to the modern reader, having been imposed over the past two centuries of medicalization which has totally devaluated the second. The latter has however become more acceptable over the last 20 years as a result of the antipsychiatric movement and its use in the work of M. Foucault, *Histoire de la folie à l'âge classique*, Paris, 1972.

that Christian thought developed a complex conception which recognized three etiological categories: organic, demonic and spiritual,
and that each of these were associated with different and specific
forms of treatment. This allows us to state from the beginning that
the widespread idea among historians, namely, that the Fathers
considered all mental illness to be the result of diabolic possession,
is completely false.

While all the schools of modern psychiatry can be seen as reductive, the Church Fathers have the merit of embracing the three
dimensions of the human being: body, psyche, and spirit. And even
though the phenomena of insanity reflects the deepest aspects and
even the most profound values of the human being, as is admitted
more and more today, the Fathers have unfailingly seen this in
terms of man's relationship with God and as tied to the development of the entire human being. Reference to the spiritual plane
constantly informs their understanding of illness, and it is this reference that assures a conceptual unity and coherence, despite the
diversity of levels encompassed and despite, at first glance, the
impression of having been pieced together. From this point of view
the idea that Byzantine society only had confused notions about
insanity and no publicly recognized[1] therapeutic system of treatment also seems debatable.

First of all the Fathers were quick to recognize that some forms of
mental illness had organic causes. For these they recommended
such appropriate medical therapy as was available in their days. This
should be stressed even though their comments in this regard are
sparse and thus give the impression that their understanding was
limited. And this remains true even if the theories and practices of
medicine in their day seem primitive and have subsequently been
abandoned. On the one hand, this demonstrates how wrong is the
prejudicial view that holds that the Fathers always blamed mental
illness on supernatural causes. On the other hand this corrective
risks supporting the purely naturalistic concept of mental disease
that the organo-mechanistic concept of psychiatry holds to, and

---

1. Cf. M. Dols, 'Insanity in Byzantine and Islamic Medicine', in J. Scarborough
(ed.), *Symposium on Byzantine Medicine, Dumbarton Oaks Papters*, 38, 1984, p137.

which derives ultimately from Hippocratic medicine. Confronted with the idea that sees mental illness as purely corporeal, the Fathers insisted on the existence of a psychological factor. But, having based themselves on an anthropology in which the soul, while closely connected to the body, retains a certain independence with respect to it, they saw mental illnesses, in cases where an organic cause was at work, as disorders of the soul's corporeal expression more than the soul itself. This is not unimportant since it allowed them, in theory, to affirm and maintain the integrity of a human being, and, in practice, to justify the absolute respect which is his due.

Secondly, the Fathers believed in the possibility of demonic causes being exerted on the psychic level, either directly or through the intermediary of the body.

Such a concept would appear shocking to those aware of the evil and sinister attacks on witches during the sixteenth and seventeenth centuries. But the beliefs and practices of the Fathers had nothing to do with such things. The Fathers, as we will show, considered the possessed not to be accomplices of the devil,[1] but rather victims, and as such entitled to special attention and solicitude.

The possibility of demonic causes may appear archaic and old-fashioned. The role of devils in the modern West is, if not ignored, at least greatly underestimated. And this is true even among Christians despite the innumerable references in the Scriptures, liturgical texts, and Patristic writings, to say nothing of the lives of the saints.

However, disregarding a certain number of factors bound up with those times, this possibility does not seem to be without value.

In the first place, just as with previously discussed physical maladies,[2] so also in mental illnesses, it should be clear from the Gospels and the writings of the Fathers that, when diabolical causes were considered, they were not ignorant of natural causes, as is often maintained, since the same illnesses were explained on either physical or diabolic grounds according to the case.

---

1. Historians are in agreement in recognizing that it was only after the fifteenth century that such confusions arose in the West. See Y. Pelicier, op. cit., p26. F. Alexander and S. Selesnick, op. cit., pp69 and 87.

2. See our *Theology of Illness*, pp95–97.

Secondly, it should be noted that such a universally recognized scholar as Marcel Sendrail, writing as a physician, did not hesitate to say in his recent *Histoire culturelle de la maladie*[1] that

current attitudes prefer to explain symptoms that are similar in their manifestation (as for example the cases of possession reported in the Gospels) as being due to mental illness rather than as having any occult basis. It remains to be seen whether or not this hypothesis is applicable in every psychopathological situation. After two thousand years, just as the tenor of so-called clear human thinking has changed, so too the modes of its alienation and perversion. One would like to continue to be convinced that the history of our own enlightened times authorizes us to deny the possibility of evil influences playing a role in the world.[2]

Thirdly, we need to recognize that, in their accounts, some of the mentally ill mention the presence, at least at times, of a strange, inner influence which incites them to certain thoughts, words, or deeds against their will, and some of them present this influence as a demonic entity which suggests clearly negative behavior with respect to themselves and/or others, even murder or suicide. Some American psychiatrists, troubled by the constancy and the similarity of these recollections among individuals from vastly different socio-cultural and even areligious backgrounds, have been led to break with the naturalist outlook that refuses to see in these situations anything other than delirium. They have been led to take these manifestations seriously and have decided as a working hypothesis to consider demonic experiences as real, or in other words to consider them as corresponding to an objective reality.[3]

1. Ed. Privat, Toulouse, 1980, p169.
2. The author recalls this passage from Baudelaire: 'More than once I was the victim of these crises and impulses which lead one to believe that malicious demons insinuate themselves in us and, without our being aware of it, accomplish in us their absurd desires' (*Petits poèmes en prose*, 'Le Mauvais Vitrier').
3. These researches are reported by Mgr. Chrysostomos in his article 'Demonology in the Orthodox Church: A Psychological Perspective', *The Greek Orthodox Theological Review*, 33, 1988, pp 45–61.

Having recorded, examined and compared the 'voices' that the patients claim to have heard, one of these psychiatrists has shown that these 'messages' are not chaotic, inconsistent or confused in nature as might be expected from a disordered psychological state, but appear to correspond to a defined intention which is logical, coherent and marked by an identifiable pattern independent of the patients.[1] Despite the boldness of his hypothesis, and given its purely descriptive nature, clearly we cannot conclude from this that demonic powers as envisioned by Christian tradition actually exist. Yet the similarity between aspects of the pattern thus brought to light and those that Christianity generally attributes to demonic activity is quite striking, with an impulsive lewdness and a relentless will to do harm being the most obvious.[2] And so it is that Mgr. Chrysostomos, after reviewing the new orientations and the latest psychiatric research concludes that

> it seems to me that it would be fruitful . . . to reassess the Patristic cosmology of the Eastern Church and draw from it a psychological model that can encompass the reality of demons and the effects of demonic forces on human behavior, both normal or psychopathic.[3]

The Fathers also held to a third etiology, namely mental illness resulting from spiritual problems, generally defined as one or another of the passions developed to an extreme. This category is most important because it pertains to the majority of the nervous conditions in present-day standard nosography, as well as some of the psychoses. Thus the attitude designated by modern psychiatry as the 'over-estimation' or 'hypertrophy of the self', highly accentuated in psychotic paranoia and to a lesser degree in neurotic hysteria, and to which many interpersonal problems—a symptom present in virtually all neurotic states—can be linked, clearly corresponds to the pride described by the Fathers. In the same category, what since Freud has been commonly called 'narcissism' likewise

1. See W. Van Dusen, *The Presence of Other Worlds*, New York, 1974.
2. See Ibid., p120.
3. 'Demonology. . .' p58.

seems to correspond to this passion, but is even more closely tied to the primal passion of 'philautia', the passionate love of oneself which has the body as its primary object. Anxiety and anguish, present in most psychoses and in all the nervous conditions, can also be easily connected with the passions of fear and sadness as conceived by the eastern Christian ascetics. Aggression, also found in the majority of neurotic states and in certain psychoses, can be connected with the passion of 'anger' in the broader sense given to this term by the Fathers. Asthenia or lethargy, common to many mental diseases, corresponds rather exactly to one of the essential components of the passion of *acedia*. One can also perceive a direct connection between standard neurotic phobias, defined as 'agonizing fears', with the passion of 'fear'. The neurosis of anxiety can be easily classified within the framework of this same passion of fear and the passion of sadness. Psychotic depression has a connection on the one hand with acedia and on the other with 'despair', an extreme form of the passion of sadness.

The nosology and therapy of spiritual maladies elaborated by the Fathers is of great interest today. First of all it represents the cumulative experience and fruit of many generations of ascetics who have explored the depth of the human soul and have come to a knowledge of even its innermost recesses in great detail; at the same time, they have spent their entire lives in mastering and transforming the soul and have acquired a unique and remarkably efficacious experience.

Secondly, they envisioned man in all his complexity, taking into account the many dimensions of his being, including the problems posed by his very existence (especially its meaning), his overall destiny and his relationship with God. The importance of these factors in the etiology and therapy of mental illness has recently been rediscovered by those involved in existential psycho-therapies.[1]

---

1. See especially: V. Frankl, *La Psychothérapie et son image de l'homme*, Paris, 1970; *The Unconscious God: psychotherapy and theology* (New York: Simon and Schuster, 1975). W. Daim, *Transvaluation de la psychanalyse*, Paris, 1957. I. Caruso, *Existential Psychology: from analysis to synthesis*, trans. E. Kraff (New York: Herder & Herder, 1964); *Psychanalyse pour la personne*, Paris, 1962. Also see C.G. Jung, *La Guérison psychologique*, Genève, 1953.

We have previously devoted a lengthy study to the subject of spiritual maladies.[1] As a result, we will limit ourselves in this work to merely recalling the analysis of the passions of acedia and sadness—their links with the various forms of depression are quite obvious and, in recent years, have attracted the attention of some psychiatrists who have shown themselves quite sensitive to the depth, richness and wisdom of Patristic analysis.[2]

These last mentioned illnesses have an exemplary value. All the more so as symptoms of anxiety and depression afflict over two hundred million individuals,[3] who most often receive only chemical treatment for their illness.[4] Undoubtedly some of these are organic in origin and, as such, this therapy is justified. However, most of them, as is generally admitted, are suffering from what is currently called 'mal de vivre' ('feeling lousy').[5] In other words they suffer from existential problems which standard psychiatry remains totally incapable of treating. It is obvious that these problems to a great extent relate to the spiritual sphere as envisioned by the Fathers whose nosology and therapeutic techniques would appear to be most pertinent, for despite the fact that both time and social context are different, they touch upon universal dimensions of human existence, upon difficulties that afflict everyone who desires to find a meaning for existence and to harmonize their interior life; individuals who

1. *Thérapeutique des maladies spirituelles*, 4th ed., Ed. du Cerf, Paris, 2000.

2. See especially J. Alliez and J. P. Huber, 'L'Acédie ou le déprimé entre le péché et la maladie', *Annales médico-psychologiques*, 145, 1987, pp393–407. B. Lecomte, *L'Acédie: invention et devenir d'une psychopathologie dans le monde monastique*, thèse de doctorat en medicine université de Nancy, I, 1991. This last study partly inspired our previous work.

3. *Le Monde*, Nov. 4, 1981, p11. 'All the epidemiological studies show that in the western countries, one in four individuals are afflicted with one of these forms of moral suffering during the course of their life.' (ibid.) In 1985 seven million French citizens could be considered depressed (cf. *Le Monde*, 1 Feb., 1985, p14).

4. In 1981, eight million tons of tranquilizers were consumed annually in the world (*Le Monde*, Nov., 4, 1981, p11). In France prescriptions for antidepressants exceeded 4,300,000 in 1997 and 7,300,000 in 1982. (*Le Monde*, Feb. 1, 1985, p14). With regard to 1991 statistics, one out of four consumed tranquilizers at least once a year in France.

5. Cf. Dr. Escoffier-Lambiote, 'Mal de vivre et médicalisation systématique. Sept millions de Francais dépressifs', *Le Monde*, Feb, 1, 1985, p14.

wish to conform their activities to values whose disappearance, as many psychiatrists and psychologists admit, leads to the increase of mental problems, especially anxiety and depression.

Another aim of this work is to present the attitude of the great saints toward 'fools', an attitude animated in particular by the Christian ideal of charity. This attitude seems to be of current interest in the way of viewing the relationships of the mentally ill with their welcome by a world where, as already pointed out, their 'oddness' remains disturbing to others and most often still incurs misunderstanding and rejection, where being confined is the only possibility open to them, and where, even in the setting of a specialty hospital, they are still, in most cases, considered to be 'patients,' consigned to the lot of a medical treatment seen as the only possible remedy, a situation which in fact objectively leads to their being considered 'chronic' and therefore abandoned.

The concern of the Fathers, such as St Theodosius, to actively engage the mentally ill in their own healing bears witness to the respect and confidence afforded them. They refused to consider them as simple patients totally subject to the therapist's control or dependent on the results of an external therapy. These concerns are similar to the most recent forms of treatment, and, in fact, several aspects of their care remind us of those previously mentioned attempts at 'therapeutic communities'.

Before examining in detail the different etiologies recognized by the Fathers, the therapeutic methods used by them, and their attitude towards those afflicted with mental illness, it is absolutely necessary to have some idea of the anthropological bases underlying their conceptions. To be precise, we must explain the manner in which they viewed the human psyche and its relationship to the body as well as the spirit.

Moreover, it seemed that we could not end this work without mentioning a very special form of folly known to Eastern Christendom, even if it is something that pertains to the ascetical rather than the psychopathological realm, namely the 'fools for Christ'. And seeing this folly simulated for spiritual ends juxtaposed with authentic forms of madness will help us better understand the nature and the purpose of an often misunderstood phenomena.

A study of 'the fools for Christ' will also provide useful insights into the manner in which insanity and the insane were viewed in Byzantine society. As we will see, the situation was not idyllic. In this society as in many others, the fool was an object of scorn and rejection except for the great saints, who show us that, even in an officially Christian society, the acceptance, respect and welcome afforded to those who were different and weak could only be the fruit of a self-conquest and a victory over the passions which allow the love of men to triumph, a love owed first, according to God, to the most destitute

The 'fool for Christ', a type of ascetic that has disappeared today, had an exemplary value. One of the motivations for this was to share in everything the conditions of the poor, the humiliated, the scorned and the social outcast, especially the 'fool', and, by an intimate experience of their state, to be better able to empathize with their ills, to draw so close to their condition so as to be of greater assistance, becoming imitators of the Apostle who said, 'I am made weak with the weak in order to gain over the weak. I become all things to all men, that I might save all' (1 Cor. 9:22).

1

ANTHROPOLOGICAL BACKGROUND: THE HUMAN COMPOSITE

BODY AND SOUL

THE FATHERS OFTEN INSIST that the human being is neither body nor soul in isolation, but entirely and indissociably both.

By affirming that the body is an integral part of the very being of man, by recognizing that the body has the same dignity as the soul,[1] and by refusing to attribute to the body an origin or a destiny different than that of the soul,[2] the Fathers contradicted the spiritualist conceptions. These conceptions viewed the body as only an *avatar* of the soul, proof of its fallen nature, a source of impurity and a tomb (*soma-sema*)[3] which accidentally imprisons the soul; as something inessential and added on to the soul. For them the essence of a person is to be found in his soul which reveals itself as one progressively negates the body and becomes detached from it.[4]

---

1. So much the more so since the Word, by becoming incarnate, assumed not only a soul, but a human body.

2. At death, the body is only separated from the soul while awaiting the resurrection which will transform it and once again unite it with the soul to partake of the blessings of the Kingdom of Heaven, or the pains of Hell.

3. Cf. Plato, *Gorgias,* 493A; *Cratylus,* 400C.

4. Gnosticism cannot be summed up in a few schools. It is a vast movement with multiple roots which has developed in many different directions. But it is certain that it is to some degree linked to Platonism (see S. Pétrement, *Essai sur le*

Correlatively, by affirming that a human being is at once soul and body,[1] they opposed every form of materialism and naturalism that denied the soul or reduced it to being an epiphenomena of the body, or something derived from and determined by the body, a point of view that sees the body as the essence of the human being and the principle source of all human activity.[2]

St Justin writes: 'Is the soul by itself man? No; but the soul of man. Would the body be called man? No, but it is called the body of man.'[3] And St Iranaeus says: 'For that flesh which has been moulded is not a perfect man in itself, but the body of a man, and part of a man. Neither is the soul itself, considered apart by itself, the man; but it is the soul of a man, and part of a man.'[4]

---

dualisme chez Platon, les gnostiques et les manichéens, Paris, 1947), at least with the Platonism of the first centuries of Christianity. The anthropology of the early Fathers (especially Iranaeus, Hippolytus, Tertullian, and even Clement of Alexandria) took shape in reaction to gnosticism and the dualistic aspects of Platonism (See M. Spanneut, *Le stoïcisme des Pères de l'Église de Clément de Rome à Clément d'Alexandrie*, Paris, 1957, pp 43, 133, 149, 150). The defense of orthodox anthropology continued to be necessary during the course of the following centuries when certain Gnostic theses, related to Originist ideas in particular, became a danger even within the Church (especially in some monastic communities). Thus it was that Origin, Evagrius and Didymus were condemned at the Fifth Council in the year 553 for having, as was once again recalled in canon 1 of the Quinisext Council in 692, 'reintroduced . . . Greek myths.' But Originism left traces beyond the sixth century; thus we see St Gregory Palamas obliged to again make clear the orthodox conception of man in the fourteenth century, and recall the Patristic teaching on the common destiny of the soul and the body in the process of deification. On the Originist crisis, see A. Guillaumont, *Les 'Kephalaia gnostica' d'Évagre le Pontique et l'histoire de l'origénisme chez les Grecs et les Syriens*, Paris, 1962, and J. Meyendorff, *Le Christ dans la théologie byzantine* (Paris: Cerf, 1969), chap. 3, pp 59–89.

1. See for example St Gregory of Nazianzus, *Discourse*, XLV, 8. St Maximus, *Mystagogy*, V, PG 91, 672D.

2. St Athanasius of Alexandria, for example stated: 'Thus each human being has a soul, a reasoning soul. It is necessary for those of little understanding to demonstrate this with a few words, the more so as some heretics deny this and imagine that the human being consists of nothing other than what we visibly apprehend, namely his body.'

3. *On the Resurrection*, no. 7.

4. *Against the Heresies*, V, 6, 1.

The human being is then both body and soul and consists of these two at once, compounded of two substances. The Fathers never tire of repeating that the human being is by his very nature made of these two components and can never be reduced to only one or the other. His very essence consists of these two elements. Thus St Irenaeus tells us, 'men ... are compound by nature, and consist of a body and a soul.'[1] St Athanagoras teaches that 'man is double, being made of body and soul,'[2] and 'is composed of these two.'[3] St Cyril of Jerusalem clearly states: 'Man is two-fold by nature, composed of a soul and a body, and it is the same God that created both the body and the soul.'[4] St John Chrysostom tells us 'man is a reasoning animal who is composed of two natures, of a spiritual soul and a material body.'[5] And St Gregory of Nyssa: 'What does the human being teach us? Body and soul at the same time, or one or the other alone? All the evidence points to the union of these two which is characteristic of the living person.'[6] And let us quote St Gregory Palamas: 'The title of human being is not applied to the soul or the body as separate entities, but of the two together, for they were created together in the image of God.'[7]

The affirmation of this double constitution, the coexistence of these two components and their clear distinction, is not to be construed however as a dualist conception. As St Gregory of Nyssa stresses, 'Man is one by nature, being made of body and soul together.'[8]

It is as a single entity with two natures especially since the soul and the body were created by the same act and at the same moment. 'The being of a person can only have one common origin,' writes St

---

1. *Against the Heresies*, II, 13, 3. Cf. *On the Apostolic Preaching*, 2.
2. *On the Resurrection*, 18.
3. *Ibid.*, 25.
4. *Catecheses*, IV, 18.
5. *Homilies on Genesis*, XIV, 5.
6. *Homilies on Pascha and the Resurrection*, III.
7. *Prosopopoea*, PG 150, 1346IC. One could also cite: St Maximus the Confessor, *Ambigua*, 7, PG 91, 1109CD. St Symeon the New Theologian, *Practical and Theological Chapters*, II, 23 and III, 62.
8. *On the Making of Man*, XXIX, 1; PG 44, 233D.

Gregory of Nyssa.[1] As St Nicetas Stethatos explains,

> The divine Word, far from establishing that either one or the other of the two natures existed previously; that either one or the other was the basis, the cause or the effect of the other—either the body in connection with the soul or vice versa—to the contrary has united the two natures without any confusion into a single unique substance.[2]

St Gregory of Nyssa affirms:

> As far as the creation of each individual is concerned, one principle does not precede the other; neither the soul comes before the body, nor the other way around.[3] . . . It is a truth that neither the soul exists before the body, nor the body apart from the soul, but the two have a common origin. If one considers these things on a supernatural level, this origin is founded primarily on the will of God; from a less elevated point of view, this occurred at the very moment of our entrance into the world.[4]

St Maximus affirms just as clearly that, at the moment of creation, the body and soul were created simultaneously and human nature is composed of a single entity:

> In its creation every composite nature, as far as its components are concerned, possesses its own parts simultaneously in this creation;[5] . . . its parts are contemporaneous to each other insofar as they coexist from the moment of their creation. Neither of the two parts pre-existed in time.[6]

---

1. Ibid. Chapters XXVIII and XXIX are specifically concerned with the refutation of the Origenist doctrine regarding the pre-existence of souls. Cf. *On the Soul and the Resurrection*, XLVI, PG 46, 113BC. St Gregory of Nyssa attacks this doctrine of metempsychosis (*On the Making of Man*, XXVIII, 232A).
    2. *On the Soul*, 14. Cf. 26 and *Letters*, IV, 9.
    3. *On the Making of Man*, XXIX, PG 44, 233D.
    4. Ibid., 236B.
    5. *Letters*, XII, PG 91, 488CD.
    6. Ibid. Maximus develops his argument on this point in *Ambigua*, 42, PG 91, 1321D–1341C. He directs his comments as much against the Origenists who affirmed the pre-existence of the soul, as against those who on the basis of a literal exegesis of

St Maximus affirms that the parts are necessarily connected to something and are both simultaneously needed to form the genus (*eidos*) of a complete human being.[1] Even death, as St Maximus stresses, only separates body and soul in a relative manner. Neither soul nor body can exist in isolation then, but are always the body and the soul not only of a given man, but of each and every man considered as a whole of which they remain parts.[2]

These brief comments show us that the Fathers constantly tried to defend a state of equilibrium in their understanding of the nature of the human being. The two substances of which he is composed are distinguished without being separated, and united without any confusion. As St Symeon the New Theologian says, the soul is united to the body 'in an inexpressible and indetectable way, and blended without mixture or confusion.'[3] And so it is not possible to totally envisage the one without the other, to see man through one independently of the other; each one, however, preserves its own nature and, in a certain measure, its own destiny.[4]

The intimate connection of soul and body implies that they act simultaneously in every human activity and partake of the same emotions. According to Nemesius of Emesa,

> the sympathy that exists between the two shows that they are united, for the whole animate being experiences one same feeling as a single entity.[5] [He further adds that] The Soul, being numbered among the things that can change, seems to have feelings

---

Exod. 21:22 affirm its postexistence. He also refutes the doctrine of metempsychosis (Cf. *Ambigua*, 7, PG 91, 1100D–1101A). See M.–H. Congourdeau, 'L'Animation de l'embryon humain chez Maxime le Confesseur', *Nouvelle revue théologique*, 111, 1989, pp 693–709 and E. Stephanou, 'La Coexistence initiale de l'âme et du corps d'après saint Grégoire de Nysse et Maxime l'Homologète', *Échos d'Orient*, 31, 1932, pp 304–315.

1. See *Ambigua*, 7, PG 91, 1100C.

2. See Ibid., 1101A–C.

3. *Practical and Theological Chapters*, II, 23. Also see Nemesius of Emesa, *On the Nature of Man*, III, PG 40, 597A.

4. Cf. St John of Damascus, *On the Orthodox Faith*, III, 16. St Issac the Syrian, *Ascetical Homilies*, 3.

5. *On the Nature of Man*, III, PG 40, 597A.

in common with the body because of its close bond with it. At the same time the soul seems to be subject to the influence of the body which can impress itself on her.[1]

'What pain or pleasure or movement is not a common activity of both body and soul?' asks St Gregory Palamas.[2] St Maximus is even more explicit:

> Every composite nature normally and necessarily involves its components, one with the other. Such is the case with men as with every composite nature. The soul without wishing involves the body and is influenced by the body. It provides the body with life without having chosen to do so and is under the body's influence, partaking of its passions[3] and sorrows through that faculty capable of receiving them.[4]

The Fathers stress the connection between body and soul and their common activity in sin. 'In every action they are, as it were, riveted together and participate equally in the end result. How then can you separate one from the other when you admit that they are joined in all their activities. And how can you put the entire responsibility on the soul when the actions involve both parties?' asks St Gregory of Nyssa.[5] The Fathers, in accord with these ideas, considered the passions[6] to be shared with the body and the soul, and also held the same to be true of the virtues.[7]

Thus it follows that every movement of the soul is accompanied by a movement of the body and every movement of the body by that of the soul.[8] Each and every act of the human being is at one

---

1. Ibid., 601B.
2. *Triads*, II, 2, 12 [p 51 Eng. ed.]. See also St John of Damascus, *On the Orthodox Faith*, II, 12.
3. Here we are speaking of the natural passions.
4. *Letters*, XXII, PG 91, 488CD.
5. *Homelies on Pascha and the Resurrection*, III.
6. It is a matter of the culpable passions as opposed to the virtues.
7. See for example St Maximus, *Centuries on Charity*, II, 57. St John of Damascus, *On the Orthodox Faith*, II, 12.
8. St Isaac the Syrian notes on this topic, while affirming that 'the movement of one is separate from the movement of the other,' and 'the will of one from the will of the other': 'through God's inscrutable wisdom, by nature the soul has been made

and the same time an act and movement of both the soul and the body. Evagrius calls attention to this double relationship.[1] St Maximus speaks very clearly to the issue:

> The following four things are said to change the body's temperament and through it to produce either impassioned or dispassionate thoughts in the intellect: angels, demons, the winds and diet. It is said that the angels change it by thought, demons by touch, the winds by varying, and diet by the quality of our food and drink and by whether we eat too much or too little. There are also changes brought about by means of memory, hearing and sight—namely when the soul is affected by joyful or distressing experiences as a result of one of these three means, and then changes the body's temperament. Thus changed, this temperament in its turn induces corresponding thoughts in the intellect.[2]

It is in the nature of the human being that no element can act without the other being implicated. The body without the soul is helpless,[3] and vice versa, but for different reasons: the body has need of the soul to live and move,[4] while the soul has need of the body to manifest, express itself, and act on the external world.[5] For the body is the servant, the organ and instrument of the soul.[6] The

---

a sharer in the body's griefs, by reason of the union of her movement with the body's movement' *Ascetical Homilies*, 3. On the union of the soul with the movements of the body, see also: Evagrius Ponticus, *Chapters on Prayer*, 63 and 68. St Maximus the Confessor, *Questiones et dubia*, 149; *Centuries on Charity*, II, 85 and 92.

1. 'Whereas others derive their reasonings and ideas and principles from the changing states of the body, yet God does the contrary. He descends upon the spirit himself and infuses his knowledge into it as he pleases. Calm peace he brings to the body's disturbed state through the spirit.' (*Chapters on Prayer*, 63).

2. *Centuries on Charity*, II, 92 (*The Philokalia*, vol. 2).

3. See St Nicetas Stethatos, *On the Soul*, 56.

4. See Nemesius of Emesa, *On the Nature of Man*, II. St Nicetas Stethatos, *De l'âme*, p 56.

5. See Gregory of Nyssa, *On the Making of Man*, XV, PG 44, 177C.

6. See St John Chrysostom, *Homilies on Genesis*, XIV, 5. Nemesius of Emesa, *On the Nature of Man*, II. St John of Damascus, *On the Orthodox Faith*, II, 12. St Nicetas Stethatos, *On the Soul*, 62.

body is absolutely necessary for the exercise of the soul's function in relation to the world and for it to manifest its powers under terrestrial conditions. With regard to this all of the activities of the soul, insofar as they are manifest, cannot exist without the body.[1]

The soul is incapable of expressing itself without the corporeal organs necessary for the realization of its activity. Such, according to Gregory of Nyssa, is the case even with an embryo where these organs are not as yet developed. 'Even if the soul does not manifest itself by certain activities, it is nevertheless present as in an embryo. In effect, the constitution of a human being which will develop, is already present, but in a hidden manner because it cannot manifest itself except by means of the necessary order of things. Thus it is present, but invisible. It will only appear thanks to the exercise of its normal activity as the body develops'; 'the activities of the soul develop along with the formation and perfection of the body that is its instrument.'[2] This is also the case, as we shall see later, with adults whose disease affects the organs and impedes them from actualizing certain potentialities of the soul. But this is true during the first years of life, when the soul, that possesses from the moment of birth the totality of its possibilities, can only manifest these in proportion to the development of the organism. St Gregory of Nyssa writes thus:

> The soul, even if does not manifest certain activities in broad daylight, is nevertheless present in the embryo. . . . It is present but invisible; it only shows itself thanks to the exercise of its natural activity which is associated with the development of the body.[3] . . . The activities of the soul develop in correlation with

---

1. It can even be said that the state of the soul is completely inscribed in the body, and especially on the face. It is this, as St John Cassian remarks, which allows the saints 'to recognize his interior state from the look, the face, the bearing of a person" (*Conferences* VII, I) The author of Ecclesiasticus as we have noted says: 'The heart of a man shows in his face, be it good or bad' (Sirach 13:25). Cf. St John Climacus, *The Ladder*, XXX, 17.

2. *On the Making of Man*, XXIX, PG 44, 236CD and 237B. Cf. 237C.

3. Ibid., 236C.

the formation and perfection of the body which is its instrument.[1]

All this should not let us forget that the soul, being incorporeal, has a different nature than the body[2] and is superior to it.[3] It is the soul that gives life to the body: the body receives from the soul its organization while the soul directs the activity of the body and maintains its unity.[4] The intimate relationship between soul and body is due to the fact that the soul penetrates each part of the body and uses its members as its organ. St Maximus notes:

The whole soul permeates the whole body and gives it life and motion. At the same time the soul is not divided or enclosed in it, since the soul is simple and incorporeal by nature. It is wholly

---

1. Ibid., 237B. Cf. 337C: 'For as the body proceeds from a very small original to the perfect state, so also the operation of the soul, growing in correspondence with the subject, gains and increases with it. For at its first formation there comes first of all its power of growth and nutriment alone, as though it were some root buried in the ground; for the limited nature of the recipient does not admit of more; then, as the plant comes forth to the light and shows its shoot to the sun, the gift of sensibility blossoms in addition, but when at last it is ripened and has grown up to its proper height, the power of reason begins to shine forth like a fruit, not appearing in its whole vigor all at once, but by care increasing with the perfection of the instrument, bearing always as much fruit as the powers of the subject allow.' The vocabulary utilized by Gregory clearly indicates that it is the activity of the soul which grows—not the soul itself. All the powers of the soul are there but their operation (or their activity) is only progressively achieved. One should not see in this a reflection of the Aristotelian theory of progressive animation (of the vegetative, sensitive and animal soul). As for St Maximus the Confessor, he explicitly opposed this last theory and affirmed without any ambiguity the presence in man of the reasonable soul from the moment of conception, for this is the distinguishing mark of the human being, and man is such (and not a plant or animal) from this moment of creation (see *Ambigua*, 42, PG 91, 1337C–1340A).

2. St Maximus the Confessor demonstrates this in detail in his *Letter* VI, PG 91, 424C–433A. See also Nemesius of Emesa, *On the Nature of Man*, III, PG 40, 597A.

3. See among others: St Athanasius, *Against the Heathen*, 32, PG 25, 64C–65A; St Maximus, *Centuries on Charity*, I, 7.

4. See St Maximus, *Ambigua*, 7, PG 91, 1100AB; 42, 1336C–1337B. St John of Damascus, *On the Orthodox Faith*, II, 12. St Nicetas Stethatos, *On the Soul*, 24. St Gregory Palamas, *Topics of Natural and Theological Science*, 3, 30 (*The Philokalia*, vol. 4).

present to the entire body and to each of its members. The body is of such a nature that it can make place for the soul by an inherent power that is receptive to the soul's activity.[1]

St Makarios teaches that:

The soul, which is a subtle body, has enveloped and clothed itself in the members of our visible body, which is gross in substance. It has clothed itself in the eye, through which it sees; in the ear, through which it hears; in the hand, the nose. In short, the soul has clothed itself in the whole visible body and all its members, becoming commingled with them, and through them accomplishing everything it does in this life.[2]

Nemesius of Emesa brings all these aspects together:

The soul is incorporeal, and yet it has established its presence in every part of the body . . . on the one hand, the soul preserves its own unity of being, and on the other, it modifies whatever it indwells, in accordance with its own life, while itself suffering no reciprocal change. For, as the presence of the sun transforms the air into light, making the air luminous by uniting light with air, at once maintaining them distinct and yet melting them together, so likewise the soul is united to the body and yet remains distinct from it . . . the soul is incorporeal, and not circumscribed to a particular portion of space, but spreading entire throughout; like a sun that spread wherever its light reached, as well as throughout the body of the sun, not being just a part of the whole that it illuminates, as would be the case if it were not omnipresent in it. For it is not the body that masters the soul, but it is the soul that masters the body. Nor is the soul contained in the body, as if in a vessel or bag. It might rather be said that the body is in the soul.[3]

1. *Ambigua*, 7, PG 91, 1100AB [*On the Cosmic Mystery of Jesus Christ. Selected Writings from St Maximus the Confessor*, trans. P. M. Blowers and R.L. Wilken (Crestwood, NY: St Vladimir's Seminary Press, 2003), p71].

2. *St Symeon Metaphrastis Paraphrase of the Homilies of St Makarios of Egypt*, 67 (*The Philokalia*, vol. 3). Cf. St Athanasius, *Against the Heathen*, 32, PG 25, 64C–65A.

3. *On the Nature of Man*, III, PG 40, 597A.

The fact that the soul governs the organization and function of the body only signifies to a certain degree the mastery of its body by the human subject. To define the degree of this mastery requires that one define the complex nature of the soul. This definition also allows us to be clear as to what degree the soul is independent of the body.

SPIRIT, SOUL AND BODY

The Fathers usually distinguish three 'powers' in the human soul.[1]

The most elementary level (which is not always explicitly distinguished and is often found included in a broader concept of the second level) corresponds to the vegetative or vital power which all living beings possess, be they human, animal or vegetable.[2] The function of this power is nutrition, growth and generation.[3] It is this which is the source of life in the organism and assures the individual functions of the vital organs.[4] The vital organs that are linked to the vegetative soul are not under the control of the human will. They function 'whether we want them to or not.'[5]

At the second level is found the 'animal' power and this power is common to both men and animals.[6] Along with the vegetative functions, it constitutes the irrational part of the soul. It is also

---

1. See St Gregory of Nyssa, *On the Making of Man*, XXIXX, PG 44, 237C. Nemesius of Emesa, *On the Nature of Man*, XV. St Maximus, *Centuries on Charity*, III, 32. St John of Damascus, *On the Orthodox Faith*, II, 12. St Nicetas Stethatos, *On the Soul*, 31–32.

2. The souls of the last two are limited to this level.

3. See St Gregory of Nyssa, *On the Making of Man*, VIII, PG 44, 144D–145A; C. St Maximus, *Centuries on Charity*, II, 32; St John of Damascus, *On the Orthodox Faith*, II, 12; St Nicetas Stethatos, *On the Soul*, 31–32

4. See St John of Damascus, *On the Orthodox Faith*, II, 12.

5. Ibid. St John of Damascus makes this clear: 'Now, deaf and disobedient to reason are the vital principle, which is also called pulsating, the seminal or generative principle, and the vegetable principle, which is also called nutritive and to which also belongs the principle of growth that builds up the body. For these are governed not by reason but by nature' (ibid).

6. See *Gregory of Nyssa, On the Making of Man*, VIII, PG 44, 145A. St Maximus, *Centuries on Charity*, III, 32.

called 'appetitive'[1] and 'passible'.[2] Apart from the capacity for sensation and perception,[3] it comprises two elements: 1) 'irrascability' and 'ardor' (*thumos*) from which all kinds of aggressiveness proceeds, as well as the will in its combative dimension,[4] and 2) concupiscability (*epithumetikon*),[5] which encompasses desire, affectivity and other such urges.[6] Also attached to it is the imagination under its elementary and non-rational aspect.[7]

In the human being the exercise of the faculties can be partially controlled by reason.[8]

At the third level we find the power of reason that pertains to man and constitutes the principle characteristic of his nature, distinguishing him from all other creatures.[9] The two principle faculties are reason and, at an even higher level, the spirit (*pneuma*) or intellect (*nous*)[10] which is the principle of consciousness (in the

1. See St John of Damascus, *On the Orthodox Faith*, II, 12; St Nicetas Stethatos, *On the Soul*, 32.

2. St John of Damascus, *On the Orthodox Faith*, II, 12.

3. See Gregory of Nyssa, *On the Making of Man*, VIII, PG 44, 145A.

4. See St John of Damascus, *On the Orthodox Faith*, II, 16.

5. Platonic in origin (*Republic* IV, 444C–E), the threefold rational—irascible—concupiscable division of elements became standard in Eastern spirituality from the time of Evagrius (see especially his *Praktikos*, 86 and 89 where Evagrius follows Gregory Nazianzus). See among others: St Dorotheus of Gaza, *Instructions*, 176. St Maximus the Confessor, *Centuries on Charity*, I, 67; III, 3; IV, 15, 80; *Letters*, II, PG 91, 397A; XXXI, 625AB. St Issac the Syrian, *Ascetical Homilies*, 4. Pseudo-John of Damascus, *On the Virtues and Vices* (*The Philokalia*, vol. 2). St Hesychios the Priest, *On Watchfulness*, 126. St Philotheus of Sinai, *Texts on Watchfulness*,16. St Nicetas Stethatos, *On the Soul*, 36; *Centuries*, I, 15, 16.

6. On these divisions see especially St John of Damascus, *On the Orthodox Faith*, II, 12 and St Nicetas Stethatos, *On the Soul*, 32; 36–41.

7. See St Maximus, *Centuries on Charity*, III, 32. John of Damascus *On the Orthodox Faith*, II, 17; 18. St Nicetas Stethatos, *On the Soul*, 65, 68.

8. See St John of Damascus, *On the Orthodox Faith*, II, 12. St Nicetas Stethatos, *On the Soul*, 31.

9. This is why St Maximus recognized, contrary to Aristotle (who will be followed later by St Thomas Aquinas), that the rational soul is present from the very first instant of human life, that is, from conception. (See Ambigua, 42, PG 91, 1337C–1340B).

10. The authors of the first centuries (for example St Ignatius of Antioch, *To The Philadelphians*, XII, 2. St Irenaeus, *Against the Heresies*, V, 6, 1) utilized the word *pneuma*, following the practice of St Paul (1 Thess. 5:23). The Fathers of the

psychological as well as the moral sense) and the capacity that man has for self-determination (*autexousia*), and thus the superior aspect of his will[1] and the principle of his liberty.[2] The *nous* is also the principle of all the intellective functions. In the first place, it is the intuitive intelligence (*nous* properly speaking), the faculty of contemplation (*theoria*) and the source of all knowledge. Secondly, it is reason (*logos*) and all that proceeds from the intelligence:[3] thinking (*ennoia, dianoia*), reflection (*dianoia*), judgment (*krisis*), discernment (*diakrisis*), and interior discourse (*endiathetos logos*) from which comes both language and memory.[4]

The *nous* is the highest faculty in man and the faculty that gives him the power to command and to direct (for which reason this is often called *egemonikon*). Because of the *nous* man has the possibility to situate, master, and transcend himself.

The *nous* represents the contemplative possibilities of the human being.[5] For the Fathers it is fundamentally that which links man with God, that leads him towards and unites him with God.[6] By means of the *nous* man is objectively and in a definite manner linked to God from the moment of his creation: the *nous* is in effect

---

fourth century and the Byzantine Fathers of the later centuries adopted and preferred the word *nous* (See J. Meyendorff, *Byzantine Theology,* 2nd ed. (New York: Fordham University Press, 1979), p141. The present author thinks that this change was made in order to avoid the ambiguity which could exist with regard to the identity of the spirit, and also to affirm the created character of the human spirit). See also A.–J. Festugière, *L'Idéal religieux des Grecs et l'Évangile*, Paris, 1932, Excursus B, 'La division corps-âme-esprit de 1 Thess.', pp212–220.

1. St Maximus the Confessor developed a quite subtle psychology of the will (See especially *Opuscules théologiques et polémiques*, 1, PG 91, 12C-20A) also used by St John of Damascus (*On the Orthodox Faith*, II, 24). See also Nemesius of Emesa, *On the Nature of Man*, XXVII–XXXIII. St Nicetas Stethatos, *On the Soul*, 38.

2. St John of Damascus, *On the Orthodox Faith*, II, 12. On liberty see the excellent synthesis of the same author (II, 24; 25; 27) which is to a great extent inspired by St Maximus the Confessor (See especially his *Opuscules théologiques et poemiques*, 1, PG 91, 16B–20A).

3. See St Maximus, *Mystagogy*, A, PG 91 672D–673A.

4. See Nemesius of Emesa, *On the Nature of Man*, XII–XIV. St John of Damascus, *On the Orthodox Faith*, II, 19–20. St Nicetas Stethatos, *On the Soul*, 65; 66, 68.

5. See St Maximus, *Mystagogy*, V, PG 91, 672D, 673BC.

6. See for example, St Maximus, *Ibid*, 673AB.

the image of God in man.[1] This image can be masked or soiled by sin, but it cannot be destroyed: it is the indelible mark of man's most profound being, of his veritable nature, the *logos* or constitutive principle of which cannot be altered.[2]

The *nous* is created immortal, thanks to grace.[3] It is changeable by nature, but is capable of controlling and directing its own changes.[4] This image of God is not by nature divine. It has the possibility by the work of divine grace, after having acquired the likeness of God, of being deified.[5]

Finally, it is important to point out that, according to the Fathers, the *nous* is that which corresponds most of all in man to his person.[6] V. Lossky writes that 'it is the seat of the person, of the human hypostasis which contains in itself the whole of man's nature—spirit, soul and body.'[7]

It is necessary to point out that the 'elements' that can be distinguished in the soul do not constitute three different souls, nor three separate parts. As St Gregory of Nyssa points out, the soul is one and not divided into parts:

1. Cf. Clement of Alexandria, *Exhortation to the Heathen*, X, 98, 4. St Athanasius of Alexandria, *Against the Heathen*, 34. St Basil of Caesarea, *Homilies on the Origin of Man*, I, 6; 7. St Maximus, *Mystagogy*, V, PG 91, 673B. St John of Damascus, *On the Orthodox Faith*, II, 12. See V. Lossky, *The Mystical Theology of the Eastern Church* (Crestwood, NY: St Vladimir's Seminary Press, 1997), pp 115–116.

2. This is a leitmotive of St Maximus the Confessor. See especially his *Ambigua*, 42, PG 91, 1341D.

3. The Christian tradition is opposed on this point to the Gnostic and Platonic tradition which affirms that the intellect is uncreated and immortal by its nature. Some Christian authors such as Origin and Nemesius of Emesa, hold to this latter point of view. See J. Meyendorff, *Le Christ dans la théologie Byzantine* (Paris: Cerf, 1969), pp 74–75.

4. Cf. St Nicetas Stethatos, *On the Soul*, 48.

5. The deified man is totally deified, both body and soul. But the Fathers often affirm that the *nous* is the first to receive grace and to be transformed by grace; it is by means of its intermediary function that grace is communicated to the rest of the human composite.

6. See V. Lossky, op. cit., p 201. J. Meyendorff, *Byzantine Theology*, p 142.

7. *Loc. cit.*

We find three distinct faculties [but] let no one suppose on this account that in the compound nature of man there are three souls welded together, contemplated each in its own limits, so that one should think man's nature to be a sort of conglomeration of several souls. The true and perfect soul is naturally one.[1]

The Fathers frequently used the dichotomous body-soul model, including in the single idea of soul (*psukhe*) all its elements, and in doing so made clear their understanding of the profound unity of the soul. On other occasions they represented it by the trichotomous spirit/intellect-soul-body model. In so doing, they wished to stress the importance of man's union with God. They wished to avoid characterizing the *nous* as a faculty separate from the soul and the body: the soul (*puskhe*), St John of Damascus teaches 'does not have the *nous* as something distinct from itself, but as its purest part, for, as the eye is to the body, so is the *nous* to the soul.'[2] The *nous* has no prior existence apart from the soul, but is created at the same time and with the soul.[3]

The *nous* is not external to the body.[4] It is united to it in the same manner as the animal and vegetative soul. It is totally one with it, not one of its parts. According to St Gregory of Nyssa 'we must ... consider that the *nous* is equally in contact with each of the parts according to a kind of combination which is indescribable.'[5] And so we find the entire soul (including the *nous*) is blended with the body[6] and, as we have already seen, totally penetrates it.

As the *nous* penetrates the totality of the body, it also penetrates the totality of the animal and vegetative soul.[7]

---

1. *On the Making of Man*, XIV, 167A
2. *On the Orthodox Faith*, II, 12.
3. See St Symeon the New Theologian, *The Practical and Theological Chapters and the Three Theological Discourses* (Kalamazoo, MI: Cistercian Publications, 1982), p126.
4. See St Athanasius of Alexandria, *Against the Heathen*, 32. St Gregory of Nyssa, *On the Making of Man*, XV, PG 44, 177B.
5. *On the Making of Man*, XII, PG 44, 160D. Cf. XXIV, 173D; XV, 177B.
6. See. St Gregory of Nyssa, *On the Making of Man*, XIV, PG 44, 176B.
7. Ibid., 176A.

By this total union of the *nous* to the totality of soul and body, the entire man is made in the image of God and as a result is a hypostasis.

By this union, the body and soul receive the possibility of complete participation in the spiritual life. The *nous* has the power to bring all the other elements of the human composite under its control and of inducing them to conform to itself, to spiritualize them and communicate to them in their inmost being the divine energies which they, by their nature, are capable (*dektikos*) of receiving. It is through the medium of the *nous* that the totality of man is capable of being one with God and being deified.

The *nous* is thus the principle of the physical unity of the human composite,[1] the principle of its spiritual unity,[2] and ultimately the means of its union with God.

By means of his reasoning soul, man is master of his actions and behavior. At the same time the *nous* is the principle of his reason, it is also the principle of his will and free choice.[3]

He is thus, unlike the animals, master of his feelings. St Athanasius also notes:

How again, the eye being naturally constituted to see and the ear to hear, do they turn from some objects and choose others? For who is it that turns away the eye from seeing? Or who shuts off the ear from hearing, its natural function? Or who often hinders the palate, to which it is natural to taste things, from its natural impulse? Or who withholds the hand from its natural activity of touching something, or turns aside the sense of smell from its normal exercise? Who is it that thus acts against the natural instincts of the body? Or how does the body, turned from its natural course, turn to the counsels of another and suffer itself to be guided at the beck of that other? Why, these things prove simply this, that the rational soul presides over the body. For the body is

---

1. Cf. St Maximus the Confessor, *Ambigua*, 7, PG 91, 1100A, B.
2. Cf. J. Meyendorff, *Byzantine Theology*, pp 141–142.
3. Thus, for St Gregory of Nazianzus, 'the *nous* is the highest power in us' (*Discourse*, XXXIX, 7, PG 36, 3431B.

not even constituted to drive itself, but it is carried at the will of another.[1]

In a more general manner, St Gregory of Nyssa notes that each element of the body 'is guarded as by a sentinel, by the noetic faculty of the soul.'[2]

The reasonable soul is likewise capable of ruling the irrational parts of the soul:[3] the irascible element, the desiring element and all that is connected with the affections and the imagination. The *nous* shows itself equally capable of controlling the psychic activities of the rational soul and of ruling the constant flux of ideas and thoughts as well as memories.

Even if the soul uses the body as an instrument and depends on the body to manifest its activities in the exterior world, it remains essentially independent.[4] Even if the body cannot move without the soul, the soul remains itself.[5] On the other hand, by means of his consciousness, man can transcend the limits of the body. 'Even when united and coupled with the body,' notes St Athanasius, '[the soul] is not shut in or commensurate with the small dimensions of the body, but often, when the body lies in bed, not moving, but in death-like sleep, the soul keeps awake by virtue of its own power, and transcends the natural power of the body.'[6]

This independence of the soul is clearly manifest with death, when the body decomposes while the soul continues to live. St Athanasius writes:

[If] the soul moves the body and is not moved by other things, it follows that the movement of the soul is spontaneous, and that this spontaneous movement goes on after the body is laid aside in the earth. If then the soul were moved by the body, it would

1. *Against the Heathen*, 32, PG 25, 64C–65A.
2. *On the Soul and the Resurrection*, PG 46, col. 76–77.
3. See among others, Nemesius of Emesa, *On the Nature of Man*, XXII. St John of Damascus, *On the Orthodox Faith*, II, 12, PG 94, 928BC.
4. See Nemesius of Emesa, *On the Nature of Man*, III, PG 40, 597A.
5. See St Athanasius, *Against the Heathen*, 33.
6. *Against the Heathen*, 33. Cf. Nemesius of Emesa, *On the Nature of Man*, III, PG 40, 597A.

follow that the severance of its motor would involve its death. But if the soul moves the body also, it follows all the more that it moves itself. But if moved by itself, it follows that it outlives the body. For the movement of the soul is the same thing as its life.[1]

St Gregory Palamas develops a similar idea in showing with great precision what distinguishes a human being from an animal:

> The soul of each animal not imbued with intelligence ... does not possess life as essence, but as activity, since here life is relative and not something in itself. Indeed, the soul of animals consists of nothing except that which is actuated by the body. Thus when the body dissolves, the soul inevitably dissolves as well. ... The soul of each man is also the life of the body that it animates. ... Yet the soul has life not only as an activity but also as its essence, since it is self-existent; for it possess a spiritual and noetic life that is evidently different from the body's and from what is actuated by the body. Hence when the body dissolves the human soul does not perish with it; and not only does it not perish but it continues to exist immortally, since it is not manifest only in relation to something else, but possesses its own life as its essence.[2]

---

1. *Against the Heathen*, 33.
2. *Topics of Natural and Theological Science*, 31–32 (*The Philokalia*, vol. 4).

2

INSANITY DUE
TO SOMATIC PROBLEMS

THE FATHERS DID NOT FAIL TO RECOGNIZE that certain forms of folly or insanity had a physiological origin, and in doing so were in agreement with the medical conceptions prevalent at the time.

The psychic intoxication produced by the consumption of alcohol or drugs is proof of such an origin in certain forms of delirium or hallucination.[1] Although external to the body, these are toxic substances that give rise to psychic disorders through the body's agency. But some deliriums can also be caused by ailments intrinsic to the body. Thus fever, a symptom common to many illnesses is also a frequent cause.[2] Nemesius of Emesa attributes some aberrations of the imagination to the weakness of the anterior ventricles of the brain.[3] St Gregory of Nyssa considered inflammation of the *phrenes* to be a possible cause of delirium.[4]

> We are aware that mental aberrations do not arise from heaviness of head [drunkenness] alone, but skilled physicians declare that our intellect is also weakened by the membranes that underlie the sides being affected by disease, when they call the disease frenzy [*phrenitis*], since the name given to those membranes is *phrenes*.[5]

---

1. See Gregory of Nyssa, *On the Making of Man*, XII, PG 44, 156D; St Methodius of Olympus, *The Banquet*, V, 5–6; St John Cassian, *Conferences*, VII, 12. Theodoret of Cyrus, *On Divine Providence*, VI, PG 83, 652B.

2. See *Vie de Saint Athanase l'Athonite*, 30. St Barsanuphius, *Letters*, 483.

3. *On the Nature of Man*, XIII.

4. St Gregory of Nyssa is here referring to a Galenic tradition.

5. *On the Making of Man*, XII, PG 44, 157D.

St Gregory of Nyssa also agreed with the opinions of those who felt that mental disequilibrium was often related to a pathological condition involving the meninges.[1] The Fathers also note that some kinds of paralysis are associated with the destruction of the mental faculties and cause the individual to go 'out of his mind'.[2]

But these are only a few examples cited incidentally. The influence of the bodily organism on psychiatric disorders is not limited to these few examples.[3] 'I admit it to be true,' writes St Gregory of Nyssa, 'that the intellectual part of the soul is often disturbed by prevalence of passions; and that the reason is blunted by some bodily accident so as to hinder its natural operation.'[4] St John Chrysostom also affirmed that: 'Small changes in the constitution of the body can trouble the soul in a great number of its functions.'[5] The Fathers treated mental aberrations of this kind as they would any bodily illness.[6] The most common categories and diagnoses in Byzantine medicine were essentially those of the Hippocratic-Galenic tradition.[7]

---

1. See *On the Making of Man*, XII, PG 44, 156D. Among the physical disorders that could cause psychic troubles, Palladius felt insomnia could be caused by excess heat or cold (*Lausiac History*, XVIII).

2. See St Barsanuphius, *Letters*, 388.

3. See John Cassian, *Conferences*, VII, 12. It is possible, as P. Canivet says (*Le Monachisme syrien selon Theodoret of Cyr*, Paris, 1977, pp141–142), that Theodoret, in the two cases of insanity mentioned in his *History of the Monks of Syria* (XIII, 9 and 13), tends to admit an organic etiology (an unspecified 'physical infirmity' in the first case, and 'a sick brain' in the second).

4. *On the Making of Man*, XII, PG 44, 157BC.

5. *Homilies on the Statutes*, II, 4.

6. Cf. T.S. Miller, *The Birth of the Hospital in the Byzantine Empire*, Baltimore, 1985, pp163–166. M.E. Keenan, 'St. Gregory of Nazianzus and Early Byzantine Medicine', *Bulletin of the History of Medicine*, 9, 1941, pp26–30; 'St Gregory of Nyssa and the Medical Profession', *Bulletin of the History of Medicine*, 15, 1944, pp154–157. On the influence of Galen on Christian society, see R. Walzer, *Galen on Jews and Christians*, Oxford, 1949.

7. On Byzantine psychiatry the principal representatives were Oribase (325–403), Aetius of Amida (502–575), Alexander of Tralles (525–605) and Paul of Egina (625–690). See F. Brunet, 'Les Médecins grecs depuis la mort de Galien jusqu'à la fin de l'empire d'Orient', in Laignel-Lavastine, *Histoire générale de la médecine*, t. I, Paris, 1936, pp433–463; G. Roccatagliata, *Storia della psichiatria antica*, Milan, 1973,

The Fathers, however, qualified these affirmations with a certain number of precisions in the light of their Christian anthropology. They distinguished them from the naturalistic categories, and avoided the errors of a deterministic, mechanist, or materialistic perspective.

---

chap. XII, pp293–311; M. Dols, 'Insanity in Byzantine and Islamic Medicine', in J. Scarborough (ed.), *Symposium on Byzantine Medicine, Dumbarton Oaks Papers*, 38, 1984, pp137–138. H. Flashar, *Mélancholie und Malancholiker in den medizinischen Theorien der Antike*, Berlin, 1966, pp118–133. (He only deals with the problem of melancholy). On ancient medicine in general, see V. Thelat, *Researches historiques sur la folie*, Paris, 1839 and A. Sémelaigne, *Études historiques sur l'aliénation mentale dans l'Antiquité*, Paris. 1869. One will find an excellent discussion of Galenic medicine presented as a continuation of Hippocratic medicine in chapter v of this work (pp182–214), in chapter XII of G. Roccatagliata's work, and also in an article by S.W. Jackson, 'Galen—On Mental Disorders', *Journal of the History of Behavioural Science*, 5, 1969, pp 365-384. The principle diagnoses of Galenic nosography are: (1) *Phrenitis* is an acute illness accompanied by fever, confusion and delirium; Galen considered it to be the result of affliction of the brain rather than of the meninges (*phrenes*). (2) *Febrile delirium* which is closely related to *phrenitis*. This was also an acute illness the cause of which was considered to affect the brain only in a second- ary manner. The delirium appears suddenly, is intermittent, of short duration, and associated with exacerbations of fever; while with *phrenitis* it develops gradually and does not go away when the fever abates. (3) *Melancholy* is a chronic non-febrile illness caused by an excess of black bile which, in the first type of this illness, affects the entire hematological system, and secondarily the brain. In a second type only the brain is affected. In a third type, called *hypochondria*, the abdominal organs and secondarily the brain are affected. It is characterized by fear, sadness, misanthropy, lassitude, and sometimes by the wish to die. (4) *Mania* is a chronic illness which affects the brain. Due to yellow bile, it is characterized by a pathological excitement and is distinguished from *phrenitis* by the absence of fever. (5) *Lethargy* is an acute malady accompanied by fever which affects the brain as well as the membranes sur- rounding the brain. It is quite similar to phrenitis, but unlike it in that it is not asso- ciated with insomnia and hyperactivity, but rather with a stuperous condition which implies a decrease in mental and physical activity. It afflicts the imagination and causes memory loss. Its cause is an excess of cold and dampness, but also an excess of corrupted phlegm. (6) *Catalepsy* (or *catochus*) is a state of rigidity and stu- por or a combination of convulsions and stupor. (7) *Epilepsy* is characterized by convulsions that affect the entire body and the cessation of psychic functions. Affecting the brain, it is caused by an accumulation of thick humors (phlegm or black bile) obstructing the opening of the median or posterior ventricles. It does not seem however to have been classified among the mental disorders but rather with *catalepsy, apoplexy,* and *hysteria* (cf. S.W. Jackson, op. cit., pp377–378).

If, on the one hand, it is admitted that an injury to or a functional defect of certain bodily organs could engender disorders in the psyche, disorders classified in certain cases among the categories of insanity, this does not mean that the soul is localized in these organs. St Gregory of Nyssa writes:

When someone says that the activity of the mind is suppressed or even disappears completely as a result of certain dispositions of the body,' writes, 'I do not see by this a sufficient proof to say that the power of the mind is restricted to a specific place.[1]

On the other hand we have seen that, according to the Patristic anthropology, the soul possess its own essence, an essence that cannot be reduced to and, strictly speaking, is not determined by the body. However the body is its organ, its necessary instrument, and does condition its activity. Without the body, the soul cannot manifest itself or realize or give expression to any of its possibilities, for it resides in the body. It is absolutely necessary that the body be in every way apt to its instrumental function, that it be in a state of health which is normal, having been ordained to this end by the Creator.[2] But if an illness attacks one of the organs of the body which the soul has need of in order to act and to manifest itself, then the psychic expression will be disturbed in a manner that accords with the trouble of its mediating organ. St Gregory of Nyssa explains one aspect of this conception by means of a standard metaphor:

Since the whole body is made like some musical instrument, just as it often happens in the case of those who know how to play, but are unable, because the unfitness of the instrument does not admit of their art, to show their skill (for that which is destroyed by time, or broken by a fall, or rendered useless by rust or decay,

1. *On the Making of Man*, XII, 160D–161A. Cf. 157D.
2. St John Chrysostom writes 'God has proportioned our body to the nobility of our soul and has made it apt to observe the soul's precepts. He did not wish to give us a body that was independent, but a body that was capable of coming to the assistance of a reasonable nature. If it had been otherwise, if it directed the operations of our soul, it would not be subject to the illnesses which it suffers' (*Homilies on the Statutes*, II, 4).

is mute and inefficient, even if it be breathed upon by one who may be an excellent artist in flute-playing); so too the mind, passing over the whole instrument, and touching each of the parts in a mode corresponding to its intellectual activities, according to its nature, produces its proper effect on those parts which are in a natural condition, but remains inoperative and ineffective upon those which are unable to admit the movement of its art; for the mind is somehow naturally adapted to be in close relation with that which is in a natural condition, but to be alien from that which is removed from nature.[1] [And again], Each organ of the human composition has its own special activity. The power of the soul can remain effective, if the organ in question is maintained in a natural and healthy condition.[2]

This conception leads to very important consequences: when psychic disorders are due to somatic problems, the soul itself is not defective, only its expression and manifestation are affected. The soul, behind these apparent disturbances is not in itself affected, but remains intact in its essence. St John the Solitary, who has recourse to the same metaphor that Gregory of Nyssa used, explains this very clearly. 'That you may know,' he states,

that the soul by its nature is separate, in the depth of its intellect, from the members of the body, and that it is by its activity through the medium of the body that it is stirred by the body's senses, mind you that when one of its interior members is injured, be it either the brain or heart, it is not the soul's nature that is impaired, but the activity exercised through these members that is impaired. When a cord in a zither, or a pipe in an organ is damaged, it is not the finger that plays upon them that is at fault, but rather it is the artistic activity of the finger that is impeded from sounding forth by the zither's cords or the organ pipe because the defects are in the instruments. The action of the hand on the musical instrument is silenced without the art disappearing from the hand nor the hand being injured. Similarly

1. *On the Making of Man*, XII, PG 44, 161AB.
2. Ibid., 164C. Cf. 164D and St John Chrysostom, *Homilies on the Statutes*, II, 4.

the knowledge of the soul is preserved within its nature, and its activity avails itself of its members. For, although it is the very nature of the soul to be revealed through the body, it might also utter a word without [bodily] admixture.[1]

This distinction used by the Fathers is of an entirely different nature than the seemingly more apt one of spirit and soul. When disorders manifest in the soul, they do not affect just the psychic 'part' of the person while the spirit remains unscathed. St Gregory of Nyssa indicates, as noted in the passages cited above, that the spirit (*nous*) is itself affected.[2] It is then the entire soul (which includes the spirit) that is affected by disorders, but it is, we repeat, only affected in its activity by means of the body. Only the *possibility* of this activity is destroyed or modified in the soul itself: the body alone impedes the normal realization of the soul and distorts its expression.[3] Such disorders have no bearing on any part of the soul or the soul's functions, but only manifest themselves in the way the soul gives expression through the body. Only the way in which the body reveals the soul and its appearance by means of the body is modified. The different powers of the soul remain in themselves unchanged and operative, and will re-manifest in a normal manner if the body is once again able to exercise its corresponding functions.

The psychiatric symptoms that present themselves in such cases are not disorders of the soul except from a very superficial point of view. The insanity which in certain of its aspects gives its name to these disorders is strictly speaking not a sickness of the soul, but of the body.[4] From this a series of important consequences follow.

First, on the basis of this understanding, one can and indeed must base one's treatment on purely physiological grounds because

---

1. *Dialogue sur l'âme et les passions des hommes*, ed Hausherr, p 68.

2. See Nemesius of Emesa, *On the Nature of Man*, XIII.

3. Nemesius of Emesa seems to agree with this position. (See *On the Nature of Man*, XIII)

4. Galenic medicine itself, because of its naturalistic character, utilized 'a purely somatic approach, so that the disturbances described were often not classified as mental illnesses.' M. Dols, 'Insanity in Byzantine and Islamic Medicine', *loc. cit*, pp 138, n 17 and 140).

the soul is not itself involved, but only what is purely somatic. As it is differentiated from other illnesses, not by nature, but by circumstance, the treatment should be undertaken, not by a 'physician of the soul', but by an ordinary doctor.

Secondly, the treatment should be aimed at returning the bodily instrument to its normal state, to reconstitute the order of nature[1] in a manner that leaves the soul intact in its essence, and thereby allow it to once again express itself normally, which is to say, without its manifestation finding itself in difficulty because of the trouble with its mediating organ.

The Fathers accepted the classification of the bodily illnesses used by the prevailing medicine of their time, namely that of the Hippocratico-Galenic system. They also adopted the principles and methods of treatment, with medications based on animal, vegetable, and mineral substances, baths and diet being the most important.[2]

But in order to justify physiological diagnosis and treatment, the evidence of an organic etiology has to be absolutely clear. To deduce this from a general and broad attitude derived from medical schools, or from presuppositions based on the dominant medical culture, or the particular beliefs of the observer is not enough. Nor should it be concluded, from those cases where psychic disorders (actually, disorders psychic in expression) appear undoubtedly caused by an organic ailment, that such is case with all possible psychic disorders. Nor can it be argued from this that the soul is determined by the body and is only an expression or epiphenomenon of the body. Simply seeing that there is a relationship between psychic

1. This is in full accord with the fundamental principles of Hippocratico-Galenic medicine according to which the illness corresponds to some sort of disequilibrium (humoral), with treatment focused on returning the body to its natural equilibrium by removing what is in excess or supplying what is lacking, according to the principle of contraries. (See M. Dols, 'Insanity in Byzantine and Islamic Medicine', loc. cit. p138.

2. See M. Dols, 'Insanity in Byzantine and Islamic Medicine', loc. cit. pp 137-1389. T.S. Miller, The Birth of the Hospital in the Byzantine Empire, Baltimore, 1985, 138, pp163–166. M.E. Keenan: 'St Gregory of Nazianzus and Early Byzantine Medicine', Bulletin of the History of Medicine, 9, 1941, pp26–30; 'St Gregory of Nyssa and the Medical Profession', Bulletin of the History of Medicine, 15, 1944, pp 154–157.

and organic disorders does not mean that one kind of disorder causes or even conditions the other. For, even if a naturalistic, materialistic, organistic, or mechanistic medicine asserts that insanity is necessarily caused by an organic disorder, the Patristic perspective, while admitting such to be true in certain cases, as we have just seen, refuses to extend this explanation to all cases; it also recognizes other possible causes, as will be seen in what follows. That the body in cases of insanity is always to some degree involved does not necessarily point to its causative or determining role, but holds to the strict relationship between the body and soul in the human composite. According to the Patristic anthropology, this relationship is, as we have seen, ambivalent. The body conditions the soul, which in the totality of the human being possess the power of command, of giving the body life and movement, and making it the constant organ of its various acts. Every action of the soul is reflected and manifested in the body. Thus somatic disorders can have their origin in the natural action of the body by the intervention of elements foreign to the soul and can inhibit or disorganize the soul's functioning without the soul being in any way troubled. But it is equally possible that what is involved on the plane of the body might have its origin in the soul itself and it is these possibilities which we must define.

Faced with the mass of psychic and somatic disorders, it is important to determine, if one kind of disorder is related to the other, just how they are related. To sort them out we should admit the possibility that psychic disorders may have an etiology that does not involve the body, while recognizing that somatic disorders, besides being possible causes, may also be only effects. Nor should we forget that, according to the Fathers, these two possibilities can be complicated by demonic influences acting on the soul either directly, or through the agency of the body. This is also something we will have to study.

Confronted by these complex and diverse multi-level etiologies, medicine finds itself surprisingly limited and its totalitarian claims cast aside. The role of medicine within this frame of reference is limited to trying to bring forth evidence of an organic cause where such is probable, and to admit that, in situations where such is not ascertainable, other possible causes exist outside its area of competence.[1]

In cases where an organic cause for a disorder is clear, the function of the physician is once more limited to the physiological level alone. By affirming that in such cases the soul in its very nature is not harmed, and hence preserves its autonomy, hampers the claim of a certain kind of medicine or psychiatry to take charge of the human soul through the body and dictate to it its own ideas and values. It is noteworthy that Tertullian denounced this meddling on the part of medicine in a realm that is by its very nature beyond its competence:

> I have looked into medical science also, the sister (as they say) of philosophy, which claims as her function to cure the body, and thereby to have a special acquaintance with the soul. From this circumstance she has great differences with her sister, pretending as the latter does to know more about the soul, through the more obvious treatment, as it were, of her in her domicile of the body. . . . To the Christian, however, but few words are necessary for the clear understanding of the whole subject.[2]

In any event, these attitudes very clearly oppose the attempt of naturalistic medicine and psychiatry to reduce the realm of the soul to physiology, to pattern the psyche's diseases after those of the body, or even to define bodily disease as disease of the psyche, thereby medicalizing all forms of insanity. Again, this negates the possibility of reducing the insane to their bodies or to clinically established symptoms, the end result being the disappearance of their true personalities behind various medical concepts. Even in cases where the organic etiology is obvious or where psychic problems viewed from the outside seem to occupy the totality of the individual's being, the Fathers tell us that the soul remains unchanged in its deepest nature,

---

1. Thus, one of the Apophthegmata inform us about the case of a young woman whose thoughts had driven her into a state of illness. The physicians 'who auscultated her said: "Perhaps she has a psychic illness, for she has no bodily illness."' As a result they declared themselves incompetent and withdrew from the case (Apophthegmata, N, 37).

2. Treatise on the Soul, 2.

intact in its essence, autonomous in its being, that it keeps watch from behind the body, immobile, silent and imperceptible, waiting for the body to be restored to a condition where the soul can once again manifest normally and express itself in its integrity which, because of illness, is withheld from view.

Here we can extend the comparison made by St Gregory of Nyssa with regard to the body, namely that illness is a mask:

> The changes produced by illness ... affect the exterior form; while the mask of the illness deforms this aspect of the person and takes its place. But, in thought, we can lift this mask and imagine what happened to Naaman the Syrian[1] and the lepers spoken of in the Gospel accounts.[2] And so the form that had been hidden by disease is once more by means of health restored to sight again with its own marks of identity.[3]

This is actually observed in many of the cases reported in the Gospels and in the lives of the saints[4] where, by a miraculous intervention, illness or insanity falls away like a mask and the person suddenly and completely returns to his normal self.

---

1. 4 Kings 5:1 seq.
2. Luke 17:12.
3. *On the Making of Man*, XXVII, PG 44, 225D–228A.
4. See St Gregory the Great, *Life of Saint Benedict*, 38. St Athanasius, *Life of Saint Anthony*, 64; 80. Theodoret of Cyr, *History of the Monks of Syria*, XXIII, 13.

3

INSANITY OF
DEMONIC ORIGIN

According to the Fathers, another cause for insanity was the direct intervention of demons. This can manifest itself in various ways and degrees, even to the extent of possession. In their eyes, the importance of such an etiology was very real, although often exaggerated. Thus André-Jean Festugière tells us:

> It was a popular belief during the fourth century of our era that demons were to be found everywhere. They were considered the cause of most illness; epilepsy of course, and every form of delirium. But we also find here the deaf and dumb, the paralytic, the hemiplegic, the person suffering from dropsy or covered with ulcers.[1]

Again, Michael Dols writes:

> Mental illness, specifically, was believed to be demonic possession. The Apostles may have distinguished it from physical illness, but the subtlety of this distinction seems to have been lost from an early time.[2]

---

1. *Les Moines d'Orient*, I, *Culture et Sainteté*, Paris, 1961, p 26.
2. 'Insanity in Byzantine and Islamic Medicine', in J. Scarborough (ed.), op.cit., pp 143–144. D. W. Amundsen and G. B. Ferngren in their study 'Medicine and Religion: Early Christianity through the Middle Ages', in M. E. Marty and K. L. Vaux (eds.), *Health/Medicine and the Faith traditions*, Philadelphia, 1982, develop a more nuanced vision (see esp. pp 97–98).

The content of the previous chapter shows these statements to be erroneous and at the same time provides us with insights into the complexity and the subtlety of the views of the Fathers. Their writings and the *Lives* of the saints repeatedly demonstrate what I have stated elsewhere[1] with regard to the New Testament accounts, namely that they distinguished quite clearly between physical and demonic etiologies, not only with regard to illnesses or infirmities of different kinds, but even for identical diseases or infirmities arising from different causes.[2] All this goes to prove that having recourse to a demonic etiology in no way indicates a naiveté of belief, an ignorance of other causes, or an inability to explain things otherwise.

We find in the Gospels a case of insanity that is clearly stated to be of demonic origin, namely that of the possessed Gerasens (Matt. 8:28–34, Mark 5:1–17, and Luke 8:26–39). Many similar cases are recorded in the *Lives* of the saints where it is clearly indicated that the mental derangement was a result of the direct action of one or more demons.[3]

The vague and general terms used to define these disorders, along with the brief descriptions usually provided, make it extremely difficult to classify them according to the complex nosological categories of current psycho-pathology, or even according to the simpler

1. *The Theology of Illness*, pp 95–98.

2. One sees this very clearly in the *Life of St Theodore of Sykeon*, where, but to cite one characteristic example, two cases of mutism are reported together, one being presented as caused by demons (chap. 94) and the other by physical causes (chap. 95). In the New Testament the only cases of mental illness (certainly this classification can be argued against from the point of view of both ancient and modern medicine) were the lunatics and epileptics. Now it is to be noted that the case related in Matt. 17:14–18, Mark 9:14–29, and Luke 9:37–43 was considered due to possession. In Mark 4:24, the lunatics are clearly distinguished from demonics which makes it obvious that they were capable of considering epilepsy as due to non-demonic causes.

3. See Callinicus, *Life of Hypatios*, XXII, 14; XXVIII, 38 seq.; XL, 1–4 and 8 seq., XLII. Cyril of Scythopolis, *Life of Abraamios*, VIII. Theodore of Petra, *Life of St Theodosios*, XVII. St Athanasius of Alexandria, *Life of Anthony*, LXIII. Theodoret of Cyrus, *History of the Monks of Syria*, XIII, 9; 13. *Life of St Theodore of Sykeon*, 129. *Vie de Saint Athanase l'Athonite*, 46.

and fewer categories in use at the time of these writings, or to establish precise comparisons.

To situate things in a general way, we can say that we are dealing either with agitated states and violent forms insanity,[1] or else, to the contrary, depressive of forms associated with lethargy or catatonia. There were many cases of delirium,[2] associated or not with the above categories or with hallucinations. Such descriptions remind us of some of the acute psychotic episodes familiar to modern nosologies. But comparisons remain hazardous, for they are both too imprecise and yet misleading by being too precise. So much has changed over the course of time in the way we understand such phenomena and hence describe them.

If the writings of the Fathers provide fewer and less precise details, and if their nosology differs from both modern as well as ancient ones, this is because they were less interested in detailed descriptions or in determining the nature of an illness from an external or clinical point of view, than in defining its basic inner and spiritual origin.[3] They were not concerned with scientific details, a concern that already characterized the medicine of their time, but rather with the essence of the problem and the spiritual meaning of the phenomena. They only recorded what made it possible to understand the attitudes, the spiritual forces, and the 'healing' power of the saints.

It is often thought today that the attribution of a demonic cause to certain forms of insanity was due to the fact that the medicine of the period was incapable of determining a natural cause. This is to forget that the medicine contemporaneous to the Patristic writings we are studying envisioned things according to the same natural perspective as modern psychiatry, and, just like the latter, left no place for demonic etiologies.[4]

1. See Theodoret of Cyr, *History of the Monks of Syria*, II, 6 (an addition to the Syriac version). Cyril of Scythopolis, *Life of Abraamios*, VIII.
2. See Palladius, *Lausiac History*, XXV; XXVI.
3. As P. Canivet remarked with regard to St Theodosius ('Erreurs de spiritualité et troubles psychiques. A propos d'un passage de la vie de S. Théodose par Théodore de Pétra (530)', *Recherches de science religieuse*, 50, 1962, p195).
4. The celebrated Hippocratic treatise entitled *On the Sacred Disease*, which

To ascribe a belief in demonic etiology to a lack of education in monastic communities[1] is to forget that some of these monks were among the most cultivated men of their times, and that several of them possessed extensive medical knowledge.[2] Some were even physicians (and some of these even continued to practice their art after becoming monks, priests, or even bishops)[3] or had received medical training at the university level.[4]

If 'profane' or 'rational' medicine chooses to ignore such a demonic etiology, this is because it accepts phenomena as the only reality that can be objectively considered. With everything subordinate to this methodology, it finds itself completely unable to understand, and is indeed obligated, by its denial of the supersensible, to explain such effects only in terms of their appearance. Such an explanation is without doubt possible since demonic action, even though it is spiritual in nature, is widely expressed in the domain of the senses and can therefore be clinically apprehended by its effects. Demonic etiologies are all the more apt to be confused with and taken for organic diseases, since they frequently manifest in bodily disorders which, externally, look like standard illnesses. In effect, demons frequently act upon the soul by means of the body, for it is the latter which is more easily and directly accessible to them. Thus they use

A.–J. Festugière considers 'one of the foundations of Greek naturalism, of western' rationalism' (Introduction to the *Vie de S. Théodore de Sykéôn*, 'Subsidia Hagiographica', no. 48, Bruxelles, 1970, p xvii), takes to task all those who would attribute to epilepsy and to mental disease in general a divine or demonic cause (chap. iii, 15).

1. See A.–J. Festugière, *Les Moines d'Orient*, i, Paris, 1961, chap. i, 'Le Moine et les Demons', pp 102–103.

2. Such as St Gregory of Nyssa and St Basil of Ancyra, Nemesius of Emesa, and St Isidore of Pelusium, or again for example Meletios (cf. our *Theology of Illness*, pp 102–103).

3. See our *Theology of Illness*, p 103.

4. Such was the case with St Gregory of Nazianzus and of St Basil of Cesarea (Cf. St Gregory of Nazianzus and early Byantine Medicine', *Bulletin of the History of Medicine*, 9, 1941, pp 8–30. M.M. Fox, *The Life and Times of St. Basil the Great as Revealed in his Works*, 'Catholic University Patristic Series', no. 57, Washington, 1939, pp 13–17.

the ordinary laws of the physical world, the same laws that can play a role in other purely physiological etiologies.

We have already seen Evagrius remark that the demons seek to alter the state of the soul and by altering the state of the body (*krasis*) and by acting on the brain.[1] But St John Cassian provides precise indications as to how the devil acts in certain cases of possession and shows how this is analogous to certain processes due to physical causes.

> When an unclean spirit makes its way into those organs in which the soul's vigor is contained, [it] imposes an unbearable and immeasurable weight on them, and overwhelms the intellectual faculties and deeply darkens their understanding. We see that this sometimes also happens through the fault of wine or fever or excessive cold or other unfavorable conditions that are externally caused. The devil, who had received power over the blessed Job's flesh, did not succeed in bringing this upon him, having been forbidden by the command of the Lord, who said: 'Behold, I hand him over to you; only spare his soul' (Job 2:6). That is to say, only do not drive him mad by weakening his soul's abode, and do not obscure the understanding and the wisdom of the one who withstands you by suffocating the governance of his heart with your weight.[2]

It appears quite clearly from this that the devil engenders psychic disturbances by provoking disturbances in the organism itself. For those limited by a naturalist perspective, and who ignore demonic intervention, there are two ways in which they can understand externally observed phenomena. First, with the clinical focus on psychic disorders most of the time, it can be tempting to define an etiology as purely psychological. But this is an illusion, for it will only grasp the intermediary and organic role of the condition that is the proximal cause, and will miss the primary cause which is demonic. Secondly, in view of the organic factors which unquestionably exist and seem to be the observable cause, it is easy for the

---

1. *Chapters on Prayer*, 68–72.
2. *Conferences*, VII, 12.

physician/psychiatrist to be unaware that they are only secondary causes and delude himself that the etiology is purely somatic. This allows him to apply treatments that are of a purely physiologic nature in all cases. Such therapy can even prove to be an asset since it unquestionably affects the involved organs. But these organs are only mediators; treatment only modifies the symptoms of the disease. Invisible to the clinician, the primary underlying cause remains present and active (how else explain the strange resistance to extremely powerful medicines), though often in changing ways (which might explain certain symptom shifts).

True, it is especially difficult to determine the presence of demonic influence, to define its manner of acting, or to gauge its importance. Such an understanding escapes the eyes of the profane.[1] Only those who have obtained the charism of the discerning of spirits from God are capable of exercising this spiritual discrimination.[2] And so such a gift presupposes a certain degree of spiritual perfection.

> Thus there is need of much prayer and of asceticism [says St Anthony the Great], that when a man has received through the Spirit the gift of discerning spirits, he may have power to recognize their [the demons'] characteristics: which of them are less and which more evil; of what nature is the special pursuit of each, and how each of them is overthrown and cast out.[3]

Although the physician/psychiatrist systematically opts for the organic hypothesis, and an observer whose outlook is not spiritual

---

1. The *Life of St Theodore of Sykeon* presents several cases of illness due to demonic influence about which the afflicted person is unaware. See chapters 71 ('a woman named Irene who for a long time had impure spirits hidden within her and was bedridden because of this, a victim of many illnesses and attacks without herself knowing that these were due the action of demons'); 84 ('a slave girl of a magnate had been possessed secretly by a demon for twenty-eight years so that she was always ill and did not know what caused the malady'); 86 ('one Peter, a merchant's son, was smitten by a demon and . . . did not know the cause of his sickness'), and 108 ('there lay a man stricken of palsy by a demon, for the unclean spirit had lain concealed in him for several years and had not shown itself').

2. See 1 Cor. 12:10.

3. St Athanasius of Alexandria, *Life of Anthony*, XXII.

might waver between a physiological and a demonic explanation,[1] such is not the case with the saints. Their faculty of discernment permits them to immediately recognize the true cause of the trouble and to distinguish between what is or is not of organic origin, what is demonic or of another nature.[2] If such a person can determine that the cause is organic, it is not because of his scientific knowledge of the body and its pathology, but indirectly by determining the absence of any non-organic cause which he is capable of spiritually knowing about in an immediate and total manner. He does not however always tell us what he sees, for what is important to him is to act, to provide a remedy.[3]

In general, when the devil cannot act directly on the soul, he will act through the intermediary of the body. He has no immediate access to the spirit of the Christian,[4] because by baptism he has lost the power that he formerly could exercise and he has been expelled from the depth of the soul where he wishes to work. He has been expelled from the depth of the soul where he formerly made his residence and has been replaced by the grace of the Holy Trinity that now surrounds the heart of the baptized.[5] As long as the baptized individual guards the grace which is in him by keeping his will turned towards God, the devil remains unable to approach his soul.[6] However, the 'bath of holiness in no way prevents the demons from attacking us.'[7] The devil attempts to seduce the soul by multiple

1. We see this in the two cases reported by Theodoret of Cyrus (*History of the Monks of Syria*, XII, 9 and 13). In the first case 'some called the illness a demonic attack, others thought it a sickness of the body'; in the second, 'a woman . . . lost her wits . . . others called it the action of a demon, while the doctors named it a disease of the brain.'

2. We find innumerable examples in the Lives of the saints where healings brought about by exorcisms are described.

3. In the two cases reported by Theodoret, one is not sure in the last analysis what the cause was. The saint consulted (Mecdonios) said nothing about this but delivered or cured two individuals.

4. Cf. Theodore of Petra, *Life of Saint Theodosius*, XLII, 12. Evagrius, *Chapters on Prayer*, 63; *The Praktikos*, 47.

5. St Diadochos of Photiki, *Hundred Chapters*, 76–79.

6. See Mark the Hermit, *On Baptism*, 22.

7. St Diadochos of Photiki, *Hundred Chapters*, 78.

suggestions that the individual however has the power to repel, by means of the divine grace which is in him.[1] 'So long as the Holy Spirit is in us,' writes St Diadochos of Photiki, 'Satan cannot enter the depths of the soul and remain there.'[2] Seeing that they cannot enter into the soul, the demons direct themselves towards the body over which they retain a certain power. As Diadochos says:

> The wicked spirits of deception are free to lurk in the bodies of those pursuing a spiritual way .., in those who are resisting and struggling against sin.[3]

This activity of the demons is allowed by God because through it the individual is tested, and by his resistance he is spiritually fortified.

> It is for a good purpose that the demons are allowed to dwell within the body, even of those who are struggling vigorously against sin; for in this way man's free will is constantly put to the test.[4] [Thus] God allows [Satan] to do this, so that a man, after passing through a trial of storm and fire, may come in the end to full enjoyment of divine blessings.[5]

It is possible for the devil to do violence to the body. Such activity is then apt to produce, as already indicated, more or less serious illnesses which can become for the individual purifying trials. 'We know,' says St John Cassian,

> that even holy men have been given over bodily to Satan or to great sufferings on account of some slight sins. For the divine clemency does not permit the least blemish or stain to be found in them on the day of judgment. . . . [God] purges away all the dross of their uncleanness in the present so that he may bring them to eternity.[6]

---

1. Cf. St Mark the Hermit, *On Baptism*, 22.
2. *Hundred Chapters*, 82.
3. Ibid.
4. Ibid.
5. Ibid., 76
6. *Conferences*, VII, 25.

Through the intermediary of the body demonic activity can, as we have said, go so far as to induce states of insanity.

But it is rare that God permits the action of the devil to achieve this in a Christian soul that has remained on a straight spiritual path. As long as he invokes God continuously, God provides him with his protection and impedes the action of Satan, preventing it from exceeding definite limits. Such is for example the case of Job as cited by St John Cassian. But such troubles most often appear as the result of some spiritual negligence. If the Christian even for a moment turns away from grace, which acts like a rampart defending his heart, he becomes once again susceptible to the power of Satan, and the latter, profiting from this relaxation, is able to introduce the seeds of disturbance into the citadel of the soul.[1]

But, if the individual turns his will away from God, no longer do the demons need to have recourse to using the body to trouble the soul. They can penetrate the soul directly because grace no longer dwells within it, and this can go so far as to result in possession.[2] St Diadochos of Photiki tells us that 'the desolation which results when God turns away from the soul allows the soul that has refused to hold on to God, to become a prisoner of the demons.' And St John Cassian notes that

> It is certain, then, that unclean spirits cannot penetrate those whose bodies they will lay hold of unless they have first possessed their minds and thoughts. And when they have stripped them of the fear and recollection of God and of spiritual meditation, they boldly attack those who are easily overcome and who are as it were bereft of all divine protection and aid, and from

1. We can show this from an example taken from St John Cassian; 'The Abba Moses . . ., was delivered over to such a dreadful demon that, once possessed by him, he would stuff his mouth with human excrement. This occurred, despite the fact that he too was a unique and incomparable man, in swift punishment for a single word that he spoke a little roughly when he was arguing with Abba Macarius' (*Conferences*, VII, 27).

2. St Diadochos of Photiki affirms that there are two kinds of demons: 'Some are more subtle, others more material in nature. The more subtle demons attack the soul, while the others hold the flesh captive' (*Hundred Chapters*, 81).

then on they make their home in them as if in property that has been handed over to them.[1]

It is when he regains possession of a soul from which he had previously been expelled that the devil manifests himself with greatest violence. He then seeks to totally bewilder the soul and in a spirit of rage, cruelty, and vengeance often produces a state of insanity: 'It is a practice of the Evil One, when he returns to someone, to make him a laughing stock so that he cannot in the future be cured.'[2] This is an evangelical teaching:

When an unclean spirit is gone out of a man he walketh through dry places seeking rest, and findeth none. Then he saith: I will return to my house from whence I came out. And coming he findeth it empty, swept and garnished. Then he goeth, and taketh with him seven other spirits more wicked than himself, and they enter in and dwell there. And the final state of that man is made worse than the first. So shall it be also to this wicked generation (Matt. 12:43–45).

Possession and the folly it engenders can quite often involve Christians who have regressed upon the spiritual path, turned away from God, and given themselves up to their passions. Thus, as Denys the Areopagite says, the possessed, like catechumens and penitents, 'can listen to the singing of the psalms and to the reading of the divinely inspired writings,' but 'may not join in the ensuing sacred acts.' As he explains, they are individuals who have formerly participated in some of the most sacred sacraments, but who, because of indolence or confusion, have fallen back into a state that is contrary to the sacraments. They

have turned away from a life conforming to divine example [he writes] and have adopted instead the ideas and character of abominable demons, are exposed to the very worst power. In their extreme folly, so destructive to themselves, they turn away from the truly real, from immortal possessions and everlasting

1. *Conferences*, VII, 24.
2. *History of the Monks of Egypt*, John of Lycopolis, 36.

bliss. They long for and work for the change and for the multiple passions characteristic of matter, for pleasures which die and corrupt, for the instability of things and for the appearance of happiness.[1]

In some cases spiritual regression is not total, and it is only because of some particular passion, or a partial straying from the path, that possession and the ensuing madness will occur to a lesser degree. The *Life of St Theodosius* provides us with an example of this. Some monks had turned from the right path by the practice of an aberrant and badly understood form of asceticism and above all, in these efforts had placed their confidence in themselves rather than God. As a result they were overcome with psychic difficulties through the activity of Satan. St Theodosius welcomed them into his monastery to care for them. St Theodore of Petra provides us with a similar case:

A number of men in the mountains and in the caves had not led the struggle for a Christian life according to Christ, and, for having practiced a rash form of asceticism with great zeal, were pierced through by the sword of pride. They had attributed their ascetic activities to their own strength and had forgotten that our Lord had said: 'Without me, you can do nothing' (John 15:5). Because of this wasting of the flesh, or having in some way fallen under the judgment of God which surpasses understanding, they were delivered up to Satan, and because of their deranged minds they could no longer control their thoughts.[2]

In a general manner one can say that the passions, insofar as they subsist in man, constitute in themselves to a certain degree a form of demonic possession. Moreover, some of the Fathers consider the seven demons spoken of in the Gospel of St Matthew cited above, as

1. *Ecclesiastical Hierarchy,* PG 3, 432C, 433D–436A. See 436B where Denys mentions 'the crowd of the possessed who are prey to their passions.'

2. *Life of St Theodosius,* 41. An analysis of this case was been made by P. Canivet in his article 'Erreurs de spiritualité et troubles psychiques. A propos d'un passage de la vie de S. Théodose par Théodore de Pétra (530)', *Recherches de science religieuse,* 50, 1962, pp161–295.

equivalent to the seven demons expelled from Mary Magdalene (Luke 8:2), and to the traditionally recognized seven passions.[1] This type of possession is a concern for every Christian in whom these passions continue in some degree to manifest themselves, and insofar as likeness to God has not been realized. For they represent in him the portion of the old man who, not as yet eliminated by grace, remains open to and manifests the influence of evil spirits. However the Christian, by the grace received in Baptism, is freed from the tyranny of the enemy[2] and always retains the power of opposing demonic activity. According to St Symeon the New theologian, baptism gives us 'freedom no longer to be held against our will in the devil's tyranny,' and 'the enemy cannot take any action against us unless we of our own will obey him.'[3] Even if, because of some unfortunate slackness, the baptized individual becomes a victim to the activity of demons, he preserves by the indelible virtue of the sacrament the power to oppose them with a categorical refusal and to turn aside his will in penitence.[4] When the soul turns again to grace, the devil will be once again expelled, even if this sometimes requires a long struggle.

But for those who are not washed in the 'waters of regeneration', the devil continues to penetrate into the depths of their souls,[5] and wields a power that cannot be overcome by anyone who relies upon their own resources. They are thus subjected to the tyranny of demonic influences and find that their thoughts and actions are controlled by them.[6] In some cases this influence goes as far as genuine possession which is not only manifested through the medium of the passions, but by an infestation of body and soul by one or

1. Notably Hermas, *The Shepherd*: Mand. II, 3; V, 2, 8; XII, 2, 2; IX, 11; X, 2; Simil. IX, 22, 3.

2. See St Dorotheus of Gaza, *Discourses*, I, 5.

3. *Practical and Theological Chapters*, III, 89 and *Catecheses* V, 447-448. Cf. 440–441.

4. See St. Mark the Hermit, *On Baptism*, 22.

5. See St Diadochos of Photiki, *Hundred Chapters*, 76

6. It is obvious that this determinism is not definitive nor is the individual without recourse: man, by virtue of the fact that he is made in the image of God which is in him, always has the possibility of turning towards God and calling upon his liberating grace.

more demons. They make such individuals, then, their plaything, driving them to behavior that can reduce them to certain categories of insanity. Such is the case of the Gerasen demons described in the Gospel (Matt. 8:28–34; Mark 5:1–20; Luke 8:26–39).[1]

It is often as difficult to say why this type of possession, accompanied with insanity and often with agitation, affects certain individuals and not others, as it is to explain why, all things being equal, a given illness afflicts one person and not another. The devil chooses to manifest himself in this manner in certain individuals for reason that are not always clear. One cannot always assume a serious sinful state with these victims, for others are spared this kind of possession whose spiritual state seems no different. And if sometimes the demonic intervention follows upon a personal sin, such, properly speaking, is more the occasion than the cause. What determines the particular choice of the demons becomes evident, however, in the case of someone who willingly and consciously delivers himself into the power of Satan (Judas being the prototype). In some cases possession and insanity have been induced by the practice of sorcery or magic.[2] Finally one can see in the person who is possessed/insane a trial authorized by God to bring about a purification and spiritual progress that, for some, could not be achieved in any other way.[3]

In every case where an individual is subject to demonic influence, God nevertheless continues to assure him of His protection by confining the extent of the demons' power within certain limits. As St John Chrysostom explains:

> Some possessed, coming out of tombs met with our Saviour. The demons begged to be permitted to enter into the body of the pigs that were in the area. Our Lord permitted this and at once the

1. However, in not every case does insanity follow upon possession.
2. St Theodoret of Cyrus, *History of the Monks of Syria*, XIII, 10 and 12. According to the Fathers, magic itself has the devil for its author. In Acts 13:10 the magician Elymas is called by St Paul 'the son of the Devil.' See St Justin: *First Apology*, 26; *Second Apology*, 5. On the position of Theodoret, see P. Canivet, *Le Monachisme syrien selon Théodoret*, Paris, 1977, p125, n37 and A. Adnès and P. Canivet, 'Guérisons miraculeuses et exorcismes dans *l'Histoire philothée* de Théodoret de Cyr,' *Revue de l'histoire des religions*, 171, 1967, p175.
3. We will return to this point later.

pigs rushed down the hill into the waters of the sea (Matt. 8:32). This is how demons behave. . . . God permitted that they should enter into this herd of pigs in order to show by example how these unreasoning animals were overwhelmed by the excessive malice of the demons that possessed them. It became clear to the entire world that, if God had not taken care to restrain their maniacal fury, the demons would act on the unfortunate possessed as they did on the pigs. So then, when you see one of these individuals acting in an agitated manner because of the devil, adore on the one hand the Lord, and the other recognize the wickedness of the hellish spirit. For the possessed offer us an example of both these things, the goodness of God and the perversity of the demon. The perversity of the demon that torments the soul in which it has established itself and the goodness of God who limits and restrains this brutal invader whose entire desire is to precipitate man into the abyss and who is prevented from using all his evil power. . . . If we were under the rule of demons we would be in no better a situation than the possessed. We would be in a worse state, for God does not leave these unfortunate victims completely under diabolic tyranny because if he did, they would suffer the most terrible evil and would not be able to endure it.[1]

CHRISTIAN ATTITUDES

What is striking about the attitude of the Fathers with regard to the possessed/insane is their positive attitude.

First of all, the possessed person is frequently not considered to be someone subject to divine chastisement, or simply suffering the natural consequence of a sinful state signifying the definitive loss of sin's victim, but someone undergoing a trial authorized by God in order to purify him and bring him to a superior spiritual state.[2] As St Paul himself indicates: 'such a one is delivered to Satan for the

---

1. *Homilies Concerning the Power of Demons*, I, 6.
2. One can in this sense understand an episode from the *Life of St Theodore of Sykeon*: 'A boy, called Arsinus, who had an unclean spirit and suffered terribly was

destruction of the flesh, that the spirit may be saved in the day of our Lord Jesus Christ'(1 Cor. 5:5). Thus with regard to the possessed, St John Cassian says:

> We ought to hold unwaveringly to two things. The first is that not one of these persons is ever tried without the permission of God. The second is that everything which is brought upon us by God, whether it appears sad or joyful at the time, is ordained as by a most tender father and a most merciful physician for our benefit. Therefore they are handed over as it were to pedagogues in order to be humiliated. Thus, when they leave this world. . . [they] may either be brought to the other life in a more purified condition or be struck with a lighter punishment.[1]

St John Chrysostom himself affirms that the ultimate meaning of demonic activity, including possession, (and clearly contrary to the devil's wishes) is in the 'correcting of man.'[2] To correct here does not mean to punish, but to 'reform,' to 'redress,' and even more fundamentally 'to convert.'[3]

The situation of those under demonic attack can even be enviable from a certain point of view, more enviable than for those in a sinful state and not subject to this kind of trial. With regard to this St John Cassian writes:

> They are to be considered really pitiable and wretched who, although they defile themselves with every crime and shameful

---

brought to him from a monastery. The Saint received him but was not anxious to cure him quickly as he said that such chastisement was beneficial to him for some time' (chap. 46).

1. *Conferences*, VII, 28.

2. *Homilies Concerning the Power of Demons*, I, 6.

3. For example, with regard to the case cited above of the Abba Moses, St John Cassian states: 'By the rapidity of his cure and through the author of the remedy the Lord showed that he had applied this purifying scourge as a grace—namely, so that the blemish of a momentary offense might not remain in him.' (*Conferences*, VII, 27) And St Theodosius says to his 'monks with deranged minds': 'Every son that the Lord approves he corrects and lashes with love. It is, I say, a sign of divine goodness that the attack of this visitation is for the correction of negligence committed during your lives.' (Theodore of Petra, *Life of St Theodosius*, 42).

deed, not only show no visible sign of diabolical possession but do not even experience a trial proportionate to their deeds or any corrective punishment. For those whose 'hardness and impenitent heart' exceeds the punishment of the present life and 'stores up for itself wrath and indignation on the day of wrath and of the revelation of the just judgment of God. . . .' (Rom. 2:5), do not deserve the quick and expeditious medicine of the present life.[1]

To the contrary, those afflicted are given the chance from now on, in the troubles that assail them, for a thorough questioning of their previous way of life, for a true purification, and for a conversion of their being which perhaps would not be possible in any other way. Having one's soul and body shaken by demonic forces can lead to the discovery of realities which had been ignored. By experiencing the terrible malice of the evil spirits in the depth of one's soul, the misery of those deprived of divine protection suddenly comes into sharp focus. These people can then, in their distress, be led to call upon God with great intensity for deliverance from the hell in which they find themselves. Withstanding, through God, every evil that must be borne, they can be purified by suffering and strengthened by patience. This hard battle that must be fought plays the role, then, of a difficult asceticism, an asceticism capable of producing spiritual transformations which, by the end, can be revealed to be extraordinary and proportionate to the unusual trials they have had to undergo.

The spiritual perspective of the Fathers views man according to his total destiny and according to their faith that everything that happens can serve for the good of his soul and his salvation. Thus the possessed/insane are not seen as utterly ruined and marked with a totally negative seal, since such a situation unlocks in certain individuals, according to their particular destinies, the possibility of

---

1. St John Cassian, *Conferences*, VII, 31. The same idea is found in the *Life of St Theodosius* of Theodore of Petra, 42–43. Let us recall that this is not a question of punishment inflicted by God. It is the person who amasses a treasury of wrath. The judgment of God only reveals to each person the extent of the evil committed and its consequences, as well as his spiritual poverty.

going beyond the disordered state in which they formerly lived and of gaining access to an awareness of realities that they would not have encountered in any other way.

It is however necessary, if these possibilities are to be effectively realized (and without which the experience of possession is totally negative), that the possessed completely disassociate himself from the demons, often made most difficult by the intensity of diabolic activity, but never impossible. Since the image of God resides permanently in every human being, freedom, an essential element of this image, is never totally annihilated and always holds out the possibility of a return to God. However, under existing conditions made exceptional and difficult because of the guile and resistance of the demons, as well as because of the clouding of the mind and the weakness of the will that they produce, it is often indispensable to be aided in this task and guided on the way by someone experienced and saintly, as will be seen below.

With regard to the possessed/insane, the Fathers manifest and recommend an attitude of profound respect.[1]

First of all, because of the previously given reason that such a destiny can hide some mysterious judgment of God and is likely to lead the individual on a path of spiritual progress, or can at least serve in some manner for his benefit. As St John Cassian says after explaining the case of the Abba Moses 'It clearly follows from this that those whom we see delivered over to different trials or to these spirits of wickedness must not be abominated or despised.'[2]

But there is yet another more general and fundamental reason. The possessed and insane individual remains a brother who has even a greater need not to be held in contempt or rejected, but on the contrary to be loved and helped since he finds himself in a condition of great suffering. As St John Cassian teaches:

We shall not only never despise them but we shall even pray ceaselessly for them as for our own members and suffer along

1. One finds numerous examples of this in the *Life of St Theodore of Sykeon*, to whom appeals for healing the possessed were frequently made.
2. *Conferences*, VII, 28.

with them from the depths of our being and with all our hearts (for when 'one member suffers, all members suffer' [1 Cor. 12:26]).[1]

The Christian should feel bound up with their destiny, believing that his own spiritual destiny is linked to theirs, as each member of the body is linked to every other member.

We cannot possibly attain to perfection without these members or ours, just as we read that our forebears were unable to arrive at the fullness of the promise without us. As the Apostle says concerning them: 'All these who were approved by the testimony of faith did not receive the promises, since God had provided something better for us so that they would not be perfected without us.'[2]

Thus, far from being excluded from the fraternal community, the possessed person, while submitting to his trials, finds himself integrated with the community through the helping attention that his particular situation of suffering and distress deserve.

It is quite evident that in the eyes of the Fathers the possessed remains a complete human being, for even though the demon occupies his body and soul, he continues to carry intact within him the indelible and unalterable image of God which constitutes his true being, his profound nature, and indeed his very humanity. In the face of this, possession is only an accident, a superficial deformity. Here again, the insanity that can result from this appears to be only a nonessential difficulty for the person assailed. It does not affect his profound nature, nor wounds it in a total or definitive manner, but allows it to subsist intact. Although externally hidden from view, his true personality always remains capable of being liberated and manifested once again. Insanity in these cases is only a provisional mask which, once removed, again makes the integrity of the individual's nature clear. The humanity of the possessed/insane is not destroyed, lost, or even altered, but simply covered over as by

1. *Conferences*, VII, 30.
2. Ibid.

a double or a parasite. The possessed/insane person, because of the image of God that subsists in him, retains the promise of the divine destiny accorded by Christ to everyone who has faith in Him. This image of God provides the possibility of approaching and of regaining the likeness. By possession/insanity the individual looses nothing fundamental to his true nature. All the spiritual possibilities remain intact, but hidden. Also, the Fathers never identified the possessed person with the demon that possessed him.[1] They knew how to distinguish the individual himself behind the power forcing him to act. As St Syncletica said with regard to an analogous situation: 'It is not he who has done the wrong, but the devil. Hate sickness, but not the sick person.'[2]

We should not therefore curse the possessed/insane as we do the devil.[3] We cannot attribute to the individual defects that essentially belong, not to him, but rather to the devils that have taken up residence in him. The possessed individual is in fact a victim who deserves the compassion of a Christian, not his judgment and condemnation. A case reported by St Athanasius of Alexandria in the *Life of St Anthony the Great* provides a telling example of the attitude of the Fathers:

> A person of rank, came to him, possessed by a demon; and the demon was so terrible that the man possessed did not know that he was coming to Anthony. But he even ate the excreta from his body. So those who brought him besought Anthony to pray for him. And Anthony pitying the young man prayed and kept watch with him all the night. And about dawn the young man suddenly attacked Anthony and gave him a push. But when those who came with him were angry, Anthony said, 'Be not

1. Except perhaps in the few cases where the deliberate will of the individual has led to his being subjected to the devil, as for example is the case of Judas about whom Christ said to the Twelve: 'One of you is a demon' (John 7:70).

2. *Apophthegmata*, alphabetical series, Syncletica, 13.

3. Historians agree in recognizing that, in the West, it is only after the Renaissance that, by an unbelievable confusion, the possessed/insane are considered the devil's accomplices, and so implicated, pursued, and penalized in 'witch-hunts'. See Y. Pélicier, *Histoire de la psychiatrie*, Paris, 1971, p26. F.G. Alexander and S.T. Selesnick, *Histoire de la psychiatrie*, Paris, 1972, pp69 and 87.

angry with the young man, for it is not he, but the demon which is in him.'[1]

There is an equally significant example in the *Life of St Athanasius the Athonite*. When a possessed/insane individual named Matthew, who had been confided to the care of a monastic brother, made things unbearably difficult, St Athanasius' reproaches were directed at the brother for his lack of perseverance but not at the possessed, for the saint knew that the difficulties he created were not truly due to him, but to the 'cruelty of the demon'. Moreover, the biographer notes that, in this case, the brothers should be struggling against the demons.[2] Similarly, when a certain Paul, seized with madness, was brought before St Abraamios and insulted the saint and God himself in a most foul manner, Cyril of Scythopolis is careful to note that 'the *demon* did not cease insulting God and pouring out abuse on Abraamios.'[3]

To say that a possessed/insane person is not responsible for his words and acts[4] is in no way a denial of his entire personality. From the Patristic point of view, the assertion of this lack of responsibility aims, to the contrary, at preserving his authentic personality, his true nature by showing that he is not identified with that which appears externally and which is in truth but the work of the devil. Nor do the Fathers put the possessed/insane person in the same category as the devil that is in him—they do not identify him with his madness. St John Chrysostom repeatedly reminds us that 'the Gospel assures us that he who calls his brother a fool will not avoid the flames of hell' (Matt. 5:22).[5] It is a serious sin to treat a man as a fool because this reduces him to what is an exterior appearance, or even an interior reality that is not part of his basic nature. Doing this reduces him to a non-essential side of himself, and blinds us as to who he really is. Doing this denies his true personality, for it is to

---

1. *Life of Anthony*, 64.
2. *Vie de Saint Athanase l'Athonite*, 46.
3. *Life of St Abraamios*, 8.
4. See St Barsanuphius, *Letters*, 101.
5. *Treatise on Virginity*, 21; Cf. *Homilies Concerning the Power of Demons*, I, 7; *Homilies on Matthew*, XVI, 8.

forget that before all else he is made in the image of God and is called to be a child of God.

The Fathers also welcomed the possessed/insane who were brought to them with great respect and treated them with love, sympathy, mercy and compassion.[1] They never treated them as guilty but always as suffering brothers. They never judged them or excluded them in any way, but admitted them with haste into their company, considering them in every way like themselves and caring for them as if they were one of their own.

Thus the already cited text by St Athanasius of Alexandria shows St Anthony 'full of sympathy' for the man brought to him. The same attitude is found with St Athanasius the Athonite and his disciples:

> Matthew was possessed by a demon. He approached the Father and begged him to help. The saint embraced him as he would a member of his own community. Then he called one of the brothers whom he know to be a skilled artisan and confided the patient to him, saying secretly: 'You will draw from this great utility and profit.' He in turn received the possessed brother into his cell as a treasure of great value.' The brother however was not able to put up with Matthew for long because of the cruelty of the possessing demon, and so 'with piety and sadness' he went to consult to St Athanasius and admit his failure and the saint held him at fault for his weakness. Matthew was then confided to a second brother 'even more skilled and generous' who also failed. He was then placed in the care of a third brother who had still greater perseverance, and the saint said to him: 'Take with you this brother and if you do not give in and become discouraged in the face of his illness, I assure you that because of your patience, you will inherit the kingdom of heaven.[2]

It is remarkable that in all these cases the possessed was welcomed and even accepted with joy. They saw in difficult cases a

---

1. 'The possessed ... inspire in us compassion and we cannot see them without bursting into tears,' notes St John Chrysostom (*Homilies on Matthew*, XXVIII, 4).
2. *Vie de Saint Athanase l'Athonite*, 46.

special occasion for practicing the virtues and being tested; a means for each person to especially exercise patience and to manifest charity. The *Life of Saint Athanasius the Athonite* clearly shows how each person tried to provide the best possible assistance for a brother afflicted with this sort of trial, and how they were saddened at not being able to do better.[1] St Hypatios also showed himself welcoming and merciful. Callinicus, in his biography tells us:

> Compassionate with all, Hypatios was loved by all. For he suffered with those who suffered and involved himself with them. To those overwhelmed by trials he said: It is written, 'Remember those who are prisoners as if you were imprisoned with them'; and concerning those mistreated, 'bear in mind that you also have a body' and 'need to cry with those who cry and rejoice with those who rejoice. . . .'[2] The saint [his biographer tells us] had pity on those who were ill, and said: 'This is one of those beaten by robbers, the demons, and who is half dead. Have mercy on him for the sake of God.'[3]

When monks developed psychic disorders due to demonic influences, Theodore of Petra tells us that St Theodosius

> welcomed them favorably, like a good father, imitating, as far as human nature allows, the mercifulness of God in the manner taught by divine precept to those who would be the disciples of Christ (Luke 6:36): 'Be ye merciful even as your father in heaven is merciful. . . .'[4] 'He is pleased with those who with greater brilliance shine forth and manifest an affectionate compassion.'[5]

The attitude of the Fathers is thus an attitude of love and paternal compassion similar to the mercy of the divine Father. Among the biographies of the saints one never sees the possessed/insane repulsed or rejected. To the contrary they were approached in a manner aimed

---

1. *Vie de Saint Athanase l'Athonite*, 46.
2. Callinicus, *Life of Hypatios*, XII, 3.
3. Ibid,. XXVIII, 57
4. *Life of St Theodosius*, XLII, 1–6.
5. Ibid., 12–13.

at integrating them within the community, treating them with at least the same regard as the other members, and considering them like sons or brothers without any reservation. The possessed/insane in no way appeared strange, foreign, or even different. They were considered no differently than other men. Nor were they set apart save for the extra charitable attention that their difficulties and sufferings merited.

Without doubt, this attitude shown by these saints was not universal beyond the spiritual milieu that their presence illuminated. For example, the *Lives* of the 'fools for Christ' show us the many ways in which such individuals were mistreated by their fellow citizens.[1] St Germanus, interviewing Abba Serenus in the seventh *Conference* of St John Cassian, asks him:

> Why do we always see them not only despised and held in horror by all but even made to abstain from the Lord's communion in our provinces, based on the words of the Gospel: 'Do not give what is holy to dogs and do not cast your pearls before swine,' when, as you say about them, it should be believed that this humiliating trial is being laid upon them for the sake of their purification and well-being.' But Abba Serenus greatly deplored such a way of thinking and acting, and considered it both a serious mistake and a grave deviation: 'We do not recall that Holy Communion was ever forbidden them. Rather, it was thought that, if possible they should be given it every day, for the words of the Gospel ('Do not give what is holy to dogs'), which you understand in an odd fashion, do not support the belief that Holy Communion becomes food for demons rather than purification and protection for body and soul. When it is received by a person it burns out as it were by a kind of fire the spirit that occupies his members and that is trying to hide in them, and it flees. It was thus that we recently saw Abba Andronicus cured. For the enemy will revile the one whom he is besieging all the more when he sees him cut off from the heavenly medicine, and

---

1. See chap. 5.

the more he thinks he is removed from the spiritual remedy the more fearfully and frequently he will make trial of him.[1]

All the Fathers are not in full agreement about this issue. St Theodosius, for example, forbids communion in the Holy Mysteries for a period time to 'monks of deranged mind.' But we have ample evidence of his profound charity and of the benevolent concern he showed these individuals to know that his attitude did not proceed from any feelings of contempt or horror. Clearly his motivations had nothing in common with those mentioned by Germanus. His attitude was rather based on the wish that those who participate in Holy Communion do so in a sufficient state of awareness, and with the thought that Holy Communion is an end and not a means. When Denys the Areopagite, describing the arrangements without doubt generally in force in the Church of his day, affirms that the possessed were not admitted to the celebration of the Holy Mysteries (the second and most essential part of the liturgy) and were forbidden to participate in Holy Communion, it was not because of any contempt of the possessed on his part, for he considered them, without any discrimination or pejorative judgment, in the same category as catechumens and penitents, and recommended that they participate in the first part of the liturgy where they might 'follow the instructions of the holy hierarchy and . . . listen to the singing of the psalms and to the reading of the divinely inspired writings.' He placed them second, ahead of the catechumens, for the possessed were different from the catechumens since they had already been participants in the holy mysteries. He simply observes that they were temporarily rendered unworthy because their state was due to the fact that, by their own fault, they had turned away from God to become prey to the passions, while the holy liturgy, rejecting even penitents, admits only those who are completely holy. It was because they were, in their particular case, the first to exclude themselves from holiness that 'the deacon charged with dividing the people' excludes them from the sacred mysteries. This exclusion was only considered temporary since the reading of the

1. St John Cassian, *Conferences*, VII, 29–30.

Holy Scriptures which the possessed were content to hear is intended to favor their conversion and lead them to rediscover the essential good from which they had turned away.[1]

No contradiction should be seen between these two preceding positions and the affirmations of the Abba Serenus. They involve, or so it would seem, somewhat different cases, and for each case it is the responsibility of the saint to discern and to decide what is the best procedure to follow, chiefly taking into account whether or not the possessed has a positive attitude with regard to the holy mysteries, and his will and capacity to participate in them with the requisite spiritual state.

The hagiographical accounts bear more than adequate witness to the welcome the possessed/insane generally received in the churches and monasteries for it to be thought as deviating from a really discriminatory overall practice.[2] The neighbors and families of those possessed and afflicted with insanity brought them to the monasteries because they were certain that they would be received with eagerness and joy, and treated with kindness and loving attention. It does not appear that such practices ever aimed at excluding such individuals from society, or imprisoning them. The monastery was not considered an asylum or prison, but a place where the possessed/insane would have the best chance of being delivered. This is because there the greatest therapeutic powers of God are invoked, and there the saints by means of their asceticism become, in the Holy Spirit, like the 'supreme and heavenly Physician', participating in his infinite compassion and regenerative Omnipotence.[3]

TREATMENT

A saint is capable not only of discerning the possible existence of a demonic intervention, but, even more, he can deliver the person so

1. Cf. *Ecclesiastical Hierarchy*, PG 3, 432C–436B.
2. Cf. M. Dols, 'Insanity in Byzantine and Islamic Medicine', pp145–146.
3. M. Dols notes that in Byzantine society, 'the mentally disturbed probably sought assistance in the monasteries, particularly in the countryside' (op. cit., p146).

affected. He is also consulted in cases of insanity of demonic origin, as well as in cases where the etiology was uncertain.[1]

The saints are known for their ability to miraculously heal all forms of mental illness, since, although the possible causes of such illnesses—and indeed all illnesses—are multiple, the spiritual remedy is unique and definitive ultimately because of the uniqueness of the Physician. Theodoret of Cyrus tells us with regard to Maron the Anchorite that God

> gave in abundance the gift of healing, with the result that his fame circulated everywhere, attracted everyone from every side. . . . One could see fevers quenched by the dew of his blessing, shivering quieted, demons put to flight, and varied diseases of every kind cured by a single remedy; the progeny of physicians apply to each disease the appropriate remedy, but the prayer of the saint is a common antidote for every distress.[2]

For it is by the power of Christ that all healing occurs and demons are expelled. The saints appeal to this power and manifest it by invoking the Name of Jesus, which is especially effective in combating demons and so can deliver men from insanity:

'The Name of Jesus can still remove distractions from the minds of men (*ekstasis dianoias*), and expel demons, and also take away diseases,'[3] declares Origin, who also tells us:

> And some give evidence of their having received through this faith a marvellous power by the cures which they perform, invoking no other name over those who need their help than that of the God of all things, and of Jesus, along with a mention of His history. For by these means we too have seen many persons freed

---

1. See Theodoret of Cyrus, *History of the Monks of Syria*, XIII, 9 and 13. A number of other examples are provided in the *Life* of the great wonderworker Theodore of Sykeon. M. Dols notes that 'consistent with the demonic nature of insanity, it would appear that most people eventually sought the aid of the Church, its saints and sacraments'; and that 'the mentally ill appear to have resorted to the churches and saints' (op. cit. p145).

2. Theodoret of Cyrus, *History of the Monks of Syria*, XVI, 2.

3. *Against Celsus*, I, 67.

from grievous calamities, and from distractions of mind (*eksta-sis*), and madness (*mania*), and countless other ills.[1]

The Name of Jesus does not however act in some automatic manner like a magical formula. Christ only responds to the use of his Name in proportion to the faith of the person who, through his Name, has recourse to his omnipotence. To master the demons in this way and put an end to their activity supposes a faith without blemish, purity of heart, profound humility, as well as a great compassion for the person who is the victim of the devil.[2] The exorcist should be truly aware, first, that what he does is not a for himself, but rather for someone who suffers and needs help, and, second, that it is not by his own power that he acts: 'to cast out demons is a favour of the Savior who granted it,' as St Anthony the Great is anxious made clear.[3] Also, all the saints when consulted, in every case and before all, resort to prayer which is the fundamental principle of 'their' treatment. They also usually make the Sign of the Cross,[4] the seal of the presence of Christ which places the individual under the grace of Christ crucified, the conqueror of every evil, of all suffering, all corruption, and the destroyer of the power of Satan. With regard to St Hypatios, Callinicus declares:

How many men driven mad (*phrenoblabesantas*) by the demons has the Lord cured through his intervention! For the Lord had given him the grace of healing to such a degree that, by his prayer and the seal of Christ [the Sign of the Cross], he expelled even the most terrible demons.[5]

The saints also had recourse to all the usual spiritual remedies for healing the possessed/insane:[6] holy oil used either by rubbing or

1. Ibid., III, 24.
2. See our *Theology of Illness*, pp99–100.
3. *Life of Anthony*, 38.
4. See for example: Callinicus, *Life of Hypatios*, XXII, 13; XL, 3. St Athanasius of Alexandria, *Life of Anthony*, 80; Theodoret of Cyrus, *History of the Monks of Syria*, XIII, 9; 13; 11, 6 (an addition to the Syriac version). *Life of St Theodore Sykeon*, 129.
5. *Life of Hypatios*, XXII, 14.
6. See our *Theology of Illness*, pp91–95.

unction, holy water,[1] and sometimes the laying on of hands.[2] The traditional form of exorcism in which a saint orders the demon to leave is only reported in a few cases.[3]

Apart from these routine and non-specific practices, some used rather special methods.

Thus, in certain cases, some Fathers had recourse to prolonged and vehement debate. This seems to have been the usual practice in the society of their times, as is indicated by the following remark by Theodoret of Cyrus:

> Specialists need to put up with difficult people, to endure those who insult them, even if struck by fists and kicked. For this how the distraught (*parapaiontes*) go too far. Physicians are not offended by such cases; they tie up the patients, forcefully dowse their heads, and invent all sorts of procedures to drive out the illness and restore the equilibrium of the body's organs.[4]

The *History of the Monks of Syria* provide us with a case of an individual brought to the Abba Julian who was possessed and who had been tied up by his neighbors.

> There was a man who had been taken over by an evil spirit and who attacked and afflicted his own body and even attacked others. Because of this possession, his associates had tied him up in a sac.[5]

This practice was not unknown to the monastic communities, since Palladius, in *The Lausiac History* tells us of two monks, Valens[6]

---

1. See for example, Theodoret of Cyrus, *History of the Monks of Syria*, XIII: 9; 13. St Epiphanius of Cyprus, *Panarion*, XXX, 10, PG 41, 422.

2. See for example Calinicos, *Life of Hypatios*, XL, 4.

3. For example, St Athanasius, *Life of Anthony*, 64. Cyril of Scythopolis, *Life of Abraamios*, VIII. *Vie de Saint Athanase l'Athonite*, XLVI. Theodoret of Cyrus, op. cit., XIII, 11.

4. *Cure of Hellenic Maladies*, I, 5, This practice is notably recommended by the Byzantine physician Paul of Aegina (cf. M. Dols, op. cit., p146, n87). Before him it was prescribed by Soranus and by Celsus (see F.G. Alexander and S.T. Selesnick, *Histoire de la psychiatrie*, Paris, 1972, p63.

5. Theodoret of Cyrus, *History of the Monks of Syria*, II, 6 (addition to the Syriac version).

6. *Lausiac History*, XXV.

and Heron[1] who under demonic influence fell into states of pride and delirium and were restrained by chains by their companions. What was the reason for this practice? While we are not given any information about Heron, we know

> the fathers bound him and put him in irons for a year and so cured him, destroying his pride by their prayers and indifference and calmer mode of life. As it is said, 'Diseases are cured by their opposites.'[2]

The restraints imposed on Valens do not seem to be in the nature of a rejection, abandonment, or something aimed at excluding him from society. The Fathers did not use this as a way of getting rid of an embarrassment, nor did they see it as inflicting a punishment. On the contrary, they were deeply concerned and persevered in their care. The indifference (*adiaphoria*) spoken of in no way signified disinterest or inattention, but was aimed at curing Valens of the pride and vanity that was the source of his delirium. Their inattention was to counteract the attention which Valens himself wished to draw to himself so that he might be an object of veneration, for he had previously, before the entire community, boasted about seeing Christ and no longer needing to receive Holy Communion.[3] One can also see this in the *Lausiac History* where similar treatment is prescribed for a certain Abraamios who, seemingly under the effect of pride and demonic activity, became delirious.

> The fathers removed him from the desert and led him to a less ascetic and calmer life, and cured him of his presumption, bringing this man who had been deluded by the demon to a knowledge of his own weakness.[4]

According to the principle indicated, 'Diseases are cured by their opposites', one must admit that in the present context the purpose of this 'restraint' was to destroy the pride of Valens (that is to lead

---

1. Ibid., XXVI
2. Ibid., XXV 5.
3. Ibid.
4. Ibid., LIII.

him, by considering his situation, to replace the pride from which he suffered with sentiments of humility), and also to isolate him for the sole purpose of leading a calmer life as mentioned, being at risk in the ordinary life of the community of having his vanity encouraged and his delirium accentuated by the presence of spectators and an attentive audience.[1]

St Hypatios himself sometimes had recourse to restraints as his biographer, Callinicus, relates in connection with a certain Zenon:

> A peasant named Zenon was brought to the servant of God. He was tormented dreadfully by a demon to the point of his not knowing where he was. He was delirious and hurled himself on everyone.... His wife in tears threw herself at the feet of St Hypatios.... Now after having received Zenon, he tied his hands and placed him in a sac without sleeves so that he was entirely enveloped with his hands tied inside [in other words a strait-jacket]. The sac was very strong. For, whenever those possessed in a dreadful manner were aggressive to the point of striking people, he would bind them in a sac to make it impossible for them to attack anyone.[2]

Doubtless, such a practice is at first shocking to those who, in our time, justly condemn all past and present forms of psychiatric restraint. Today the practice and use of the strait-jacket (which Callinicus sees as equivalent to the sac) has been all but abandoned, and so too its most recent form the chemical strait-jacket. But we are not dealing with the same thing here. Within the framework of psychiatric institutions, all these means of restraint were and are in many cases still applied without justifiable therapeutic reasons or positive goal; besides, they convey a rejection or exclusion, and are aimed at isolation as an end in itself. They abandon the 'crazy person' to himself, perpetuating the illness, and simply stifling its

---

1. Heron found himself in a similar spiritual situation: he 'was attacked by pride and flung off all restraints and cherished presumptuous sentiments against the fathers.... He even abused Scripture to serve the purpose of his folly (*moria*)' (*Lausiac History*, XVI, I).

2. *Life of Hypatios*: XXVIII: 38–39 and 48–49.

external expression to make it easier for those caring for him and for society.

The practice of St Hypatios is completely different both in context and meaning. Notice first of all that he does not apply it in a general and systematic manner. It was used only in a number of well-defined cases: those individuals 'possessed in a dreadful manner,' 'aggressive to the point of attacking people,' which is to say presenting in a truly and unquestionably dangerous state (and not just alleged to be so from a vague fear or motives of a societal nature).[1] Moreover the possessed is not a priori considered dangerous. St John Chrysostom, for example, writes that 'the possessed are not so much a danger to others, but more often to themselves.'[2] The use of restraints by St Hypatios was aimed at something far more fundamental than protection; it was not so much a means for his friends and relations to avoid the effects of the madman's frenzy, as a means to come to the aid of the one possessed. Callinicus tells us, immediately after the just cited text, that those bound in this way were 'subdued and obliged to fast and pray without ceasing, for God would heal them through the intercession of the saint.'[3] Here restraint seems to have as its chief purpose to prevent the victim of the demon from dissipating his energies in useless agitation and harmful aggression, to help hold these energies in check and keep them disengaged so as to reorient them in a positive and healing direction. Restraint made it possible to transform the energy previously expressed in agitation

1. Callinicus cites another case where chains were used, and which shows the great violence of some of the possessed: 'Another time, a young man named Stephanos was brought by his mother. He was tortured by a demon in a most atrocious manner. He could not remain in one place, but prowled about striking himself with heavy blows. He was strong and quite capable of overcoming ten men and broke the chains around his hands as if they were bits of wood. . . . The demon even tried to make him commit a murder. When his brothers took a nap in the middle of the day, he raised a heavy stool and wanted to strike their heads with it. But the Lord did not allow it. . . . One of the young brothers woke up and subdued him. There was a struggle and it was with difficulty that thirty-six men tied him up. He bit two and took a piece out of one of their arms and a finger from another.' *Life of Hypatios*, XL, 8–15.

2. *Homilies on Matthew*, XXVII, 4; see also ibid., LXXXI, 3.

3. *Life of Hypatios*, XXVIII, 49–50.

and violence into fasting and prayer. This sublimation was facilitated by the active intercession of the saint, who also rendered the fasting and prayer of the possessed more efficacious by accompanying them with his own fasting and prayer. Use of restraints seems to have had as its primary goal to allow the implementation of a so-called therapeutic program.[1] There was no intention, either in goal or effect, of inhumanly excluding or isolating the possessed/insane, since treatment was accompanied at all times by St Hypatios' watchful attention, benevolence and compassion.

In none of the cases does it appear that restraint constituted the treatment or was aimed at replacing the treatment. In every case it was a minor and subordinate practice that was clearly not used with everyone; we have only taken the time to discuss it to show that in the monastic context it had no negative significance.

Much more important it seems to us was the recourse to fasting and prayer which were truly their basic therapy. Their use is justified and even demanded in these cases by the teaching of Christ who considered such treatment more than adequate: 'This kind of demon can only be expelled by prayer and fasting' (Mark 9:29). St John Chrysostom said with regard to this:

When someone is disturbed by an impure spirit, show him the face of fasting: he freezes up and, because of his fear, remains more motionless than even the very rocks. He appears to be bound by fetters, and truly so, when he sees fasting joined together with her inseparable sister, prayer ... fasting expels the hostile foes of our salvation in this manner and is so terrible to the enemies of our life.[2]

The Fathers tried to have the possessed/insane participate, as far as possible, in their own healing, as we saw St Hypatios do with Zenon in the passage cited above. They especially encouraged them,

1. The same aim lies behind conscientious psychiatrists' use of chemical medications (a new form of restraint in current use and even called 'chemical straitjacket') as a necessary prelude to psychotherapy for the 'mentally deranged' who, because of excessive agitation, could not otherwise be treated.

2. *Homilies on Repentance*, V, 1. On the role of fasting also see *Homilies on Matthew*, LVII, 4.

as far as possible, to both fast and pray. With regard to this latter practice, the therapeutic importance of which we will point out, St John Chrysostom says:

> It is completely impossible for one who is possessed, and who lives in pleasure and among the delights of this world, to ever be delivered from the demon possessing him. Fasting is a most efficacious and necessary remedy for this kind of illness.[1]

And soon after this he points out that, while fasting has a special power, it is not sufficient but must be accompanied with prayer which can even be said to take precedence. We also know from Theodore of Petra that St Theodosius took advantage of those moments, when he found the 'monks with deranged minds' in a 'normal state' and 'in control of their faculties', to teach them what they should do, and in what way they themselves should struggle to obtain deliverance from their difficulties. St Theodosius exhorted them first of all to be patient and to hope. By these exhortations 'he restored the courage of all these monks', and so 'he delivered many from the illness they suffered and, by their own patience, they obtained healing for themselves.'[2]

But notice that the goal of St Theodosius was not healing at any price for these monks, for he considered it more useful in certain cases to have to continue to struggle and persevere in patience. Theodore of Petra tells us:

> He taught others to have courage and to hold on to the good in the face of their suffering. He in fact thought that in some of these cases it was better to be patient than to wish to be delivered from one's difficulties, for the first course of action achieved impassibility while the second proved that one lacked courage. Also he did not struggle to heal the ill person but advised him on how to hold on to the good with generosity and offer to God humble thoughts prompted by our miserable condition.[3]

---

1. *Homilies on Matthew*, LVII, 4.
2. Cf. *Life of St Theodosius*, 42–44.
3. Ibid., 44.

St Theodosius here acted as a wise spiritual father, advising and giving to each one a remedy appropriate to his own personality and particular situation, seeing in each case what would achieve the greatest good. While healing allows some to reap most important spiritual benefits, a continuation of the struggle allows others to progress and gain a higher degree of perfection. Here again we see the positive sense in which the Fathers view certain forms of psychic disorders when they are of use in bringing about a spiritual benefit in those so affected. These disorders do not have a value in themselves, nor by themselves can they be the cause of spiritual progress, but by the self-surpassing occasioned by them, a self-surpassing only made possible most often when the one stricken is guided to adopt an attitude towards them conducive to his or her well-being. St Theodosius taught these monks above all to accept their sufferings, live with them, and recognize that they could serve for their good if used correctly, that is if they could transform them by asceticism into growth in virtue. He exhorted them even to thank God for their sufferings and to embrace them as if they themselves had asked for them:

> Those who are tied to this miserable body must necessarily undergo all manner of suffering. Let us make of this a work of our own will by accepting these trials which befall us through the divine will, rejoicing always in them and giving thanks in every circumstance.[1]

In all his counsels St Theodosius led his monks to stand back a bit from their trials and discover their meaning, thus avoiding the added misery which would otherwise result from a sense of their absurdity. By revealing their usefulness and the spiritual benefits to be gained from them, they were aided in accepting them with joy, and therefore not discouraged or depressed because of them. He also gave them a means to not remain passive before them, but to transcend and master them by making them an instrument of their salvation. At the same time St Theodosius exhorted the monks to

---

1. *Life of St Theodosius*, 43–44.

persevere in prayer, for without prayer it is impossible to achieve any true good.[1]

If the Fathers tried to have the possessed/insane participate as much as possible in their own deliverance, it was because the individual must, if he is to be delivered from demonic influence, turn his will from himself and orient it towards God. God, in effect, does not grant healing unless it is asked of him, for he has created man free and in all the cases respects his will and will not act against it. However, the will of the individual is not always fully at his disposal. The cases of the monks with whom St Theodosius was working are exceptional, for their awareness was not entirely clouded by their disorders and they experienced moments of lucidity. On the other hand there were monks who, in spite of their ascetical deviations, remained fundamentally oriented towards God and thus remained accessible to the directions of the saint. To the contrary, there are cases in which those stricken with madness, whether possessed or sick, have lost consciousness of who they are and what they are doing. As St John Cassian remarks:

It is quite certain that they do not endure this incursion of spirits in only one way. Some are possessed in such a manner that they have no idea what they are doing or saying, while others know and remember afterward.[2]

Those whose consciousness is disturbed in a significant way can not even ask for their own healing or give evidence of their faith, as indicated by St Barsanuphius:

The daughter of the Canaanite woman and the servant of the centurion had lost their senses, one as a result of insanity and the other because of the torment induced by the illness, and were unable to cooperate by faith in the prayers offered up for them.[3]

And yet it is possible for such individuals to be delivered and healed thanks to the faith and the prayers of those around them or

1. Ibid., 44.
2. *Conferences*, VII, 12.
3. *Letters*, 399.

accompanying them, as well as to those of the saint to whom they are entrusted. But the power of the saint's intercession is so much stronger when the faith of those asking for the deliverance of the possessed is more ardent and their prayers more fervent. Callinicus tells us that

> Hypatios always said to everyone: 'The Lord said to the blind person: 'Do you believe I am able to do this?' If the Lord thus demands faith on the part of the person who approaches him, how much more should this be the case for us other sinners. If then you believe in my God whom I have served since my youth, and if you believe that by my prayer he will grant you healing, God will gladly grant this. If then those who bring me a sick person have only a little faith, it is not easy for the one who intercedes to be heard since the faith of the person asking does not support his prayer. If in return his faith and prayer collaborate, God hears the one who prays and grants the healing. For no one should think that without God's grace anyone can heal another person. As our Lord said: 'Heal the sick, cast out devils. Freely have you received, freely give' [Matt. 10:8]. Clearly, it is from God that those who are worthy receive the grace of healing and that it is this, working through them, that accomplishes healings.[1]

Deliverance of the possessed/insane, just like the healing of the sick, most especially in situations where such people are too feeble or powerless to do so because of their state, supposes the collaboration of relatives and even all members of the community in the prayer of the 'therapist'. Deliverance/healing presupposes a genuine solidarity in faith and compassion, all members suffering with the member who suffers (1 Cor. 12:26), each one asking deliverance in the name of the person with as much and even greater force than the person himself might have in asking for this, were he fully aware of his state and had a sufficient desire to leave it. Once again they are far from blaming the person or wishing to exclude him. On the contrary they strive for a greater union, and above all for a spiritual integration. Whether the state of the possessed/insane is the consequence of a

---

1. *Life of Hypatios*, XXVIII, 40–46.

particular personal fault or a sinful state only obliges others involved to a greater love and attention, in conformity with St Paul's recommendations (1 Cor. 12:20–25):

> But now there are many members indeed, yet one body. And the eye cannot say to the hand: I need not thy help; nor again the head to the feet: I have no need of you. Yea, much more those that seem to be the more feeble members of the body, are more necessary. And such as we think to be the less honorable members of the body, about these we put more abundant honor; and those that are our uncomely parts, have more abundant comeliness. . . . God hath tempered the body together, giving to that which wanted the more abundant honor, that there might be no schism in the body; but the members might be mutually careful one for another.

The Fathers are the first to give us an example of this solicitude and to show us how to give proof of our compassion, attention and solidarity. Thus Palladius, in his *Lausiac History*, describes how St Macarius the Egyptian fasted and prayed for seven consecutive days to free a young man from his possession/insanity.[1] We also see St Anthony the Great praying and keeping vigil all night next to a possessed person who had lost his mind.[2] Theodoret tells us about St Julian 'groaning, praying, and crying' near a man from whom he expelled a demon that had enchained him, made him distraught and bite his own flesh, and impelled him to attack others.[3] St Theodosius was consumed with tender compassion for the brothers afflicted by a deranged mind.[4] Following the example of St Paul,[5] 'he became weak with those who were weak,' as Theodore of Petra tells us.[6] And we see him have so much compassion for the state 'of the brothers who had lost their minds' that he goes so far as to

1. *Lausiac History*, XVII, 13.
2. *Life of Anthony*, 64.
3. *A History of the Monks of Syria*, II. 6 (additional to the Syrian version)
4. Theodore of Petra, *Life of St Theodosius*, 42.
5. 'To the weak I become weak, that I might gain the weak. I become all things to all men, that I might save all' (1 Cor. 9:22).
6. *Life of St Theodosius*, 44.

assume responsibility for the faults they had committed,[1] and partake of their lot, saying: 'My children, let us show to the one who sent *us* these trials for *our* salvation that we are thankful for them.'[2] He himself also shows that he participated personally in their correction by implicating himself in the advice given and the task to be performed:

> Let *us* offer the fruit of *our* patience to those who have managed to turn to us. Through this affliction make *us* worthy of approval by bringing forth a hope that does not dishonor *us*. May the rigors of this present life be for *us* a pledge of our anticipated release.[3]

The attention shown and the help brought by the Fathers to the suffering individuals over whom they took responsibility is made clear in the most elementary and banal acts of daily living. Their spiritual solicitude was also materially practiced. Thus for example we see St Hypatios with his own hands putting pieces of bread into Zenon's mouth when he refused to eat;[4] he did the same for Aetios.[5]

Another important aspect of the therapy used by the Fathers consists in the arrangements made for the material living conditions of the possessed/insane aimed at promoting their healing. Thus St Theodosius had a hesychasterion (*esukhasterion*) specially built for 'brothers with deranged minds', a place of peace and quiet (*esukhia*), 'which was like a second monastery within the monastery.'[6] This was so they could benefit from a residence sufficiently isolated from the agitations of daily life and could organize their own lives according to their particular needs.

The Fathers seem to have placed a great deal of importance on

---

1. St Theodosius said: 'The negligences which *we* have committed' (Ibid., 42, 1. 20).
2. Ibid., 43, 1.14.
3. *Life of St Theodosius*, 43, 1. 16–20. In Patristic accounts we constantly see the Fathers implicate themselves in the reproaches made and the advice given to their disciples, and use the first person plural in addressing them.
4. *Life of Hypatios*, XXVIII, 55.
5. Ibid., XII, 7.
6. Theodore of Petra, *Life of St Theodosius*, 42, 1. 6–9.

silence and rest which constituted, in certain cases, an essential element (but certainly not sufficient in itself) in their therapeutic method. Callinicus tells us with regard to one Aetios, who was 'demented (*phrenoblabes*) and also very sick physically,'[1] that Hypatios 'cared for the man, prayed for him, rubbed him with holy oil, and *arranged times of rest for him*; he did this to restore him and God cured him.'[2]

The Fathers had the possessed/insane reside in the monastery until they were cured, desiring to have them under their care at all times. By having them reside in the same place as the monks[3] (as for example St Athanasius the Athonite who lodged Matthew in the very cells of the brothers in whose care he placed him[4]), it is equally probable that they sought to integrate them into the regular cycles of the monastic life so they could acquire a more organized and materially structured existence. But also and above all this was done so that they might be continually in the calming presence of men habitually patient, full of compassion and truly charitable. In this way they could symbiotically and even unconsciously participate in their virtues. The proximity of holy individuals in the monastery could also be highly profitable because of the grace that emanates from their person and radiates some distance around them, and from the calm atmosphere which is the result of their simple outlook or from their presence alone, even when silent.[5]

Whatever the importance or even the necessity of all the conditions or therapeutic principles alluded to, it must be repeated that deliverance/healing is always obtained by the prayer of a saint; this is fundamental and indispensable. By the intercession of the saint this often occurs immediately and miraculously, and the individual finds himself totally freed from his possession/insanity, as if he had

---

1. *Life of Hypatios*, XII, 7. His dementia was not caused by a bodily illness, but by the practice of magic (see ibid., XII, 4).

2. Ibid., XII, 10.

3. See *Life of Hypatios*, XL, 13–14.

4. *Vie de Saint Athanase l'Athonite*, 46.

5. Do not forget that the simple presence of saintly people inspires a great fear in demons, causes them suffering and compels them to flee as far away as possible from such holy people. These are reasons given by St Anthony (*Life of Anthony*, 30).

never been stricken with it. Insanity and possession reveal themselves to be like masks which fall away. The *Lives* of the saints give us many examples of these miraculous deliverances. We shall cite some of them.

St Macedonius the Anchorite, in order to heal a woman afflicted with bulimia ('though eating thirty chickens a day, she could not by surfeit extinguish her appetite but hungered for still more')

came and offered prayers, and by placing his hand over water, tracing the sign of salvation [the Sign of the Cross], and telling her to drink, healed the disease. And so completely did he blunt the excess of her appetite that thereafter a small piece of chicken each day satisfied her need for food.[1]

In order to heal a woman who had lost her mind (*exo ton phrenon egegonei*) ('She could recognize none of her household, and could not bear to take food or drink. She continued delirious for a very long time.') the same saint

addressed earnest supplications. On completing his prayer, he bade water be brought, traced the sign of salvation and bade her drink it.... As she drank, she came to herself and became sane: totally freed of her affliction, she recognized the man of God, and begging to take his hand placed it on her eyes and moved it to her mouth. From then on she continued to have a sound mind.[2]

When Abba Moses, arguing with Abba Macarius, was suddenly

delivered over to such a dreadful demon that, once possessed by him, he would stuff his mouth with human excrement..., at once, thanks to the aforesaid Abba Macarius' humble prayer, the wicked spirit quickly took to flight and left him.[3]

A person named Paul 'was seized with madness.' He was brought to St Abraamios.

---

1. Theodoret of Cyrus, *History of the Monks of Syria*, XIII, 9.
2. Ibid., XIII, 13.
3. St John Cassian, *Conferences*, VII, 27.

As soon as he saw the saint the demon threw Paul on the ground and started to torment and molest him... The demon did not cease to insult God and burst out in abusive language against Abraamios.... Abraamios replied: 'In the Name of Jesus Christ I order you to quit this man and never return in any way.' The demon left and the man was healed on the spot.[1]

A certain Athelaos was molested by a dreadful demon.

This demon came upon him as a result of a most powerful charm.... Thanks to the prayers of the saint [Hypatios] the Lord made known the individuals responsible for this curse and made the demon leave the man so that he was healed and recovered his sanity.[2]

On one occasion St Hypatios went to the church of the Holy Apostles. He found there a woman tormented by a demon. 'He marked her with the Sign of the Cross and prayed. She threw herself at his feet was suddenly at peace and rising up she came to herself, for God had healed her by the imposition of the hands of the saint.'[3]

Sometimes healing is not immediate. This is especially the case when the demon tormenting the possessed person is particularly resistive. The saint's intervention then takes more time. But in all cases deliverance is not delayed very long. Here again, we will give some examples.

St Anthony delivered a possessed person that had been brought to him,[4] after spending a night in vigil at his side. Likewise In this case no trace of his troubles remained:

The young man had become whole, and having come at last to his right mind, knew where he was, and saluted the old man and gave thanks to God.[5]

1. Cyril of Scythopolis, *Life of Abraamios*, VIII.
2. Callinicus, *Life of Hypatios*, XXII, 15–20.
3. *Life of Hypatios*, XL, 1–4.
4. *Life of Anthony*, 64.
5. Ibid.

St Macarius had to fast and pray for seven days in order to dislodge from a young possessed man who 'often ate his own dirt and drank his own water' the demon who had driven him to do such aberrant things.[1]

For fourteen days a demon continued to inhabit a certain Alexander who St Hypatios had welcomed into his monastery. It was only after this that 'at last, by the prayer of the saint, the demon cried out with a loud voice and left.'[2]

Sometimes possessed/insane individuals who were cured again fell after a period of time. Thus Zenon, who St Hypatios had restrained and forced to fast and pray while praying for him himself,

was healed in a few days. [But] returning home, he soon plunged back into a disorderly and worldly life and the impure spirit returned anew. [He was once again brought to the monastery.] He remained some time and once again recovered, but again he was tormented and had to be brought back again some time afterwards. This happened four times. [After that, however] the Lord finally healed him and he gave thanks to God. Thereafter he remained in good health.[3]

Stephanos presents a similar case:

After having lived some time at the monastery, he was healed by the prayers of the servant of God [Hypatios]. He left and once again fell into the frenzied disorders of the world. This is why the demon returned to him. He was once again restrained and brought to the saint. God again healed him by his intercession. This occurred three or four times over a period of four years. Later the demon even tried to get him to commit a murder. . . . But the Lord, by the prayers of his servant Hypatios, at last healed him and the demon no longer came near him.[4]

1. Palladius, *Lausiac History*, XVII
2. *Life of Hypatios*, XL, 5–7.
3. *Life of Hypatios*, XXVIII, 53–56.
4. Ibid., XL, 10–13, 16.

We can see from these last two examples that the possessed, once delivered, risk relapsing into the diseases that afflicted them if they lead a disordered life subject to their passions, for by this they let the devil reintroduce himself. To preserve the benefit of their healing, they must place themselves under the protection of God, and then it is impossible for the demons to attack them. 'There is no way for someone to fall into an dissolute way of life without having been abandoned by the Providence of God,' St Paphnuntius declares. And St Diadochos of Photiki teaches that 'So long as the Holy Spirit is in us, Satan cannot enter the depths of the soul and remain there.'[1] St Anthony similarly explains:

> While the Lord is with us, our foes can do us no hurt. For when they come they approach us in a form corresponding to the state in which they discover us, and adapt their delusions to the condition of mind in which they find us. . . . Thus the enemy, seeing Job fortified, withdrew from him; but finding Judas unguarded, him he took captive. Thus if we wish to despise the enemy, let us ever ponder over the things of the Lord.[2]

For the 'monks with deranged minds' in the monastery of St Theodosius healing was certainly longer in coming, but demonic activity was also, in the case of the monks, more brutal than in the just cited cases, and a rapid intervention was not justified insofar as St Theodosius thought, as we have seen, that the brothers would derive a greater spiritual benefit by patiently enduring their trials than by being delivered immediately. On the other hand, they had at their disposal, contrary to the majority of the other possessed, periods of lucidity, and the saint took advantage of this to have them participate in their own healing. Thus for the most part abandoned to their own efforts (and this so that they would be strengthened), but remaining despite everything quite frail, the improvement of their condition was certainly slower than it would have been had Theodosius acted in their stead with all the power of his sanctity. This slow process had the effect of allowing the benefits to be more firmly acquired.

---

1. *Hundred Chapters*, 82.
2. *Life of Anthony*, 42.

To finish, let us note that a possessed/insane person, by his faith and his prayer in moments of lucidity, could obtain deliverance through the intercession of a saint without his visibly intervening. We see this in the case of a certain Stephanos, related by Theodore of Petra: After St Theodosius had died,

> a man tormented by an unclean spirit ceased not standing by his precious corpse, and he declared—for it so happened that, by divine Providence, he was of sound mind at that moment—that he would not leave the saint until he had obtained what he desired. ... God then, who has mercy, found the words of the supplicant acceptable, and just as he had been accustomed to producing miracles by means of his saint ... he soon delivered the man from the misery that held him. This evil spirit, in fact, after having thrown the man to the ground, was annihilated by the invisible hand of God.[1]

Someone who is possessed/insane and who, because of this state, finds himself unable to seek out any intercession, can nevertheless be healed by a saint no longer living visibly in this world, as this other example drawn from the *Life of St Benedict* shows:

> A certain woman falling mad, lost the use of reason so far that she walked up and down, day and night, in mountains and valleys, in woods and fields, and rested only in that place where extreme weariness forced her to stay. One day it so happened that, although she wandered at random, yet she missed not the right way; for she came to the cave of the blessed man Benedict, and not knowing anything, she went in and reposed herself there that night, and rising up in the morning, she departed as sound in sense and well in her wits as though she had never been distracted in her whole life, and so continued always after, even to her dying day.[2]

1. Theodore of Petra, op. cit., 95, 8–96, 16.
2. St Gregory the Great, *Life of St Benedict*, 38.

As for St John Chrysostom, he recalls

the places consecrated to the martyrs where several demoniacs, who were so enraged that they ate human flesh, have recovered and are at peace.[1]

---

1. *Consolation to Stagirius*, I, 10.

4

INSANITY OF SPIRITUAL ORIGIN

MENTAL AND SPIRITUAL ILLNESS

ALTHOUGH, FOR THE FATHERS, one category of mental illness or form of insanity had a somatic etiology, and a second category a demonic one, the third category is of spiritual origin. While the first has (our fallen) nature for its cause and the second demons, the free will of an individual is responsible for the third, even if demonic activity and our free will sometimes share responsibility in the first two situations.

Mental illnesses of spiritual origin should not be confused with the spiritual illnesses themselves. Spiritual illnesses are formed by a disorder or perversion of nature (more precisely of nature's mode of existence) in the personal relationship of the individual to God. On the psychic plane, mental illnesses correspond to somatic disorders on the plane of the body; mental illness has to do with difficulties in the psyche considered in itself, with a dysfunction of the psyche's nature considered within its natural order.

From the point of view of Patristic anthropology, such a distinction can only have a relative value, for nature can never be considered in isolation and is fundamentally defined by its relationship to God. By the will of the Creator, man naturally ordained to God in all the faculties of his being, even though he depends on his own free will to induce them to act in accord with or against nature.[1]

1. See our *Thérapeutique des maladies spirituelles*, pp 17–128.

The Patristic model of health and spiritual illness is closely connected to the manner in which these various faculties are used by man.[1]

And so it is that, for the Fathers, an important share of the disorders today considered to be purely psychic actually have to do with the spiritual realm. In this sense the nosography and treatment of spiritual illnesses embraces, but goes beyond psychopathology. In other words, mental illnesses (or symptoms) of non-organic etiology are for them dependent on a spiritual diagnosis and treatment. Having devoted a sizable treatise to this subject,[2] we will refer to this source for a more complete view of this matter and limit ourselves here to pointing out some of the relationships between the spiritual illnesses of Patristic nosography and the mental illnesses of modern psychopathology.

The prevailing ideas of psychiatry about health and mental illness have nothing absolute about them. They rely on a conception of health and normality which the antipsychiatric movement has pointed to as doubtful, showing that the models for these 'norms' are highly relative and vary according to the cultures or societies that condition their definition.[3]

The difference between Patristic and modern psychiatric nosography does not allow us to establish many or precise connections. On the other hand, even today there are well-known variations between different schools and countries in the way mental illnesses are classified and defined. The very possibility of a unified classification poses great problems.[4]

Also, connections are more possible between symptoms than between syndromes.

1. Ibid.
2. Ibid.
3. See in particular the works of R. Laing and D. Cooper. Also the works already cited of M. Foucault, *Histoire de la folie à l'âge classique*, Paris, 1972, and of M. Sandrail, *Histoire culturelle de la maladie*, Toulouse, 1980. See also M. Dols, 'Insanity in Byzantine and Islamic Medicine', op. cit., p136.
4. See H. Ey, P. Bernard, C. Brisset, *Manuel de psychiatrie*, 1974, pp215–219, H. Ey, *Études psychiatriques*, III, Paris, 1954, pp19–45. E. Stengel, 'Classification of Mental Disorders', *Bull. OMS*, 21, 1959, pp600–663.

One important difference is, on the other hand, due to the fact that modern psychiatry is based on a medical model and as such embraces a naturalistic perspective that *a priori* excludes any reference to the religious or moral domain.[1]

(1) A certain number of problems examined by standard modern nosography appear to be related to what Patristic nosology called the passion of pride. Modern psychiatry, while not unaware of the pathogenic character of this attitude, has however divorced it from its moral and spiritual dimension, most often designating it as a 'self-valorization' or 'hypertrophy of the ego'. This attitude is present to a high degree in paranoid psychoses. It is also found in hysteria. Many of the difficulties in maintaining relationships—a symptom present in the majority of neuroses—can be connected with it.

In the same order of reality is what has commonly been called 'narcissism' since the time of Freud. This also corresponds to the passion of pride, and even more to 'philautia' or the passionate love of one's self which often has the body as its primary object.

(2) The anxiety and anguish present in most psychoses as well as in all neuroses can be linked in part to what the Fathers considered to be the passions of fear and sadness.

(3) The aggressiveness to be found in the majority of neuroses and in certain psychoses can be linked to the passion of 'anger' in the broad sense as we have defined it.

---

1. We should, however, recall the interesting attempts made to use this last perspective by C.G. Jung (*La Guérison psychologique*), H. Baruk (*Psychiatrie moral expérimentale, individuelle et sociale*, Paris, 1945), V. Frankl (*La Psychothérapie et son image de l'homme, The Unconscious God: psychotherapy and theology*), W. Daim (*Transvaluation de la psychanalyse*), and I. Caruso (*Existential Psychology: From Analysis to Synthesis*). These different authors have this in common: they recognize the spiritual side of man as a component of his nature and destiny, and affirm that mental illness can only be understood relative to his destiny within the framework of his nature. It can indeed be legitimately asked to what extent a purely naturalistic psychiatry is possible, and if it does not inevitably entail an implicit anthropology and metaphysic, with just the fact of considering the human being a purely naturalistic phenomena already drawn from such presuppositions.

(4) Debility, a symptom common to many mental illnesses corresponds rather closely to one of the essential components of acedia.

(5) Depressive symptoms, to be found in many neuroses and psychoses, can be directly linked to acedia and sadness.

Apart from these symptoms, several syndromes appear to be connected to the passions in spiritual nosology.

(6) Thus neurotic phobias appear to have some connection with the passion of fear; they are moreover standardly defined as 'agonizing fears'.

(7) Anxiety neurosis can be understood in relation to the passion of sadness, but also and above all to fear.

(8) Psychotic melancholia can be to some degree connected with both acedia and sadness, especially in its extreme form of 'despair'.

(9) Without any doubt the closest and most direct relationship can be established between the acedia and sadness of Patristic nosology and the different forms of depression. Nor has this relationship failed to attract the attention of certain psychiatrists who have recently devoted several studies to this subject.[1] And its importance warrants our repeating the essentials of the analysis we have devoted to these two passions, limiting ourselves however to their psychic dimensions and effects.

---

1. See especially J. Alliez and J. –P. Huber, 'L'Acédie ou le déprimé entre le péché et la maladie', *Annales medico-psychologiques*, 145, 1987, pp393–407. B. Lecomte, *L'Acédie: invention et devenir d'une psychopathologie dans le monde monastique*, doctoral thesis in medicine, University of Nancy I, 1991. This last study, while dealing primarily with the monastic life in the East and West, goes well beyond these limits: the author shows that acedia also involves lay people and points to certain literary examples (Pascal, Kierkegaard) and establishes an interesting comparison with psychasthenia as described by Janet.

The Nosology of Sadness

Sadness (*lupe*) appears to be a state of soul which, beside the simple meaning of the word, involves discouragement,[1] debility,[2] psychic heaviness and sorrow, dejection,[3] distress,[4] oppression[5] and depression[6] most often accompanied by anxiety and even with anguish.[7]

This condition can have many causes but it always involves a pathological reaction of the soul's irascible (*thumos*) and/or desiring faculty (*epithumia*), and as such is essentially tied to concupiscence or anger. 'Sadness,' Evagrius tells us, 'tends to come up at times because of the deprivation of one's desires (*steresis ton epithumion*). On other occasions it accompanies anger.'[8] But it can also be a result of the direct action of demons on the soul, or it may even arise for no apparent reason.

Let us consider these different etiologies in detail.

First Cause—The Frustration of Desires

Evagrius tells us 'Sadness is formed from an unsatisfied carnal desire.'[9] St John Cassian likewise notes that sadness 'sometimes results when we see ourselves deceived with regard to some hope,'[10] and that one of its chief kinds follows from 'a desire that has been thwarted.'[11] In that 'every desire is tied to a passion,'[12] every passion is prone to produce sadness. According to Evagrius: 'whoever loves the world will often be sad.'[13] One can also say that pleasure is tied

1. See St John Chrysostom, *Consolation to Stagirius*, III, 13.
2. Ibid.
3. See St Dorotheus of Gaza, *Instructions*, V, 67.
4. Ibid.
5. Ibid.
6. See John Cassian, *The Institutes*, IX, 1.
7. See St Dorotheus of Gaza, *Instructions*, V, 67.
8. *The Praktikos*, 10.
9. *On Various Evil Thoughts*, 11, PG 79, 1156D.
10. *The Institutes*, IX, 4.
11. *Conferences*, V, 11.
12. Evagrius, *loc. cit.*
13. Ibid.

to desire and as Evagrius says, 'sadness is a deprivation of sensual pleasure (*steresis edones*), whether actually present or only hoped for.'[1] St Maximus[2] and St Thalassios[3] also define it in these terms. Stressing that sensual pleasure is inevitably followed by sorrow—sorrow most often being psychic rather than physical, taking in other words the form of sadness—St Maximus affirms that sadness 'is the end result of sensual pleasure.'[4]

Insofar as it results from the frustration of some carnal desire (using 'carnal' in the broad sense of this term) and its associated pleasure, sadness reveals an attachment on the part of the affected individual to sensual goods and the values of the world. This is why Evagrius stresses that it is linked to all the passions to the degree that they imply covetousness[5] and asserts: 'If we continue to cherish some affection for anything in this world it is impossible to repel this enemy.'[6] St Dorotheus of Gaza says much the same: 'If a man does not despise all material things ... he cannot ... be delivered from sorrow.'[7] St John Climacus remarks that whoever

> has come to hate the world has escaped sorrow. But [whoever] has an attachment to anything visible is not yet delivered from grief. For how is it possible not to be sad at the loss of something we love?[8]

He also notes that 'If anyone thinks that he is without attachment to some object, but is grieved at its loss, then he is completely deceiving himself.'[9]

Also, one often sees sadness provoked by the loss of some tangible good,[10] by whatever injury suffered on this same plane.[11] The

1. Evagrius, *The Praktikos*, 19.
2. See *To Thalassios*. 58, PG 90, 592D.
3. *Centuries*, I, 75.
4. *To Thalassios*, 58, PG 90, 592D.
5. See *On Various Evil Thoughts*, 11–12.
6. *The Praktikos*, 19.
7. *Maxims*, 4.
8. *The Ladder*, II, 7.
9. Ibid., 11.
10. See St John Chrysostom, *Homilies on the Statutes*, V, 4; VII, 1.
11. See St John Cassian, *Conferences*, V, 11.

passional attachment of man to his earthly life and to what it includes for the satisfaction of his passions can equally give rise to sadness in the ordeals with or thoughts about everything that might imperil it: illness,[1] all the evils to which one is exposed,[2] and death.[3]

Sadness can also result from envy of some moral or material good possessed by another.[4] It can likewise have its origin in some deception used in order to obtain honors and then is necessarily tied to *cenodoxia* (or vainglory).[5]

Again, let us note that sadness may not be provoked by the frustration of a particular desire having to do with a quite specific object; it may be tied to a more general dissatisfaction, an overall sense of frustration with one's entire life, revealing that a person's deep-seated desires (the true significance of which are not always clearly known) have not been fulfilled.

Second Cause—Anger

'Sadness,' as Evagrius teaches, 'can come from thoughts of anger.' In effect, he explains, 'anger is a desire for vengeance and unsatisfied vengeance produces sadness.'[6] St Maximus says the same. '[Sadness] is linked with rancor. When the intellect forms the image of a brother's face with a feeling of resentment, it is clear that it harbors rancor against him.'[7] St John Cassian also affirms this without going into details: '[sadness] sometimes follows upon the vice of anger'[8] and he further notes that a kind of sadness 'is begotten once anger has ceased.'[9]

---

1. St John Chrysostom, *loc. cit.*, VII, I.
2. Ibid.
3. Ibid., and V, 4. St Gregory of Nyssa, *On Virginity*, III, 3 and 9.
4. See St Maximus, *Centuries on Charity*, III, 91.
5. See St Isaac the Syrian, *Ascetical Homilies*, 1. Evagrius, *On Various Evil Thoughts*, 12, PG 79, 1158B.
6. *On Various Evil Thoughts*, II PG 79, 1156BC. Cf. *Praktikos*, 10, and 25.
7. *Centuries on Charity*, III, 89. Cf. 96.
8. *The Institutes*, IX, 4.
9. *Conferences*, V, 11.

Sadness can occur in connection with feelings other than rancor: it often results from the feeling that one's anger was excessive or disproportionate to what had stimulated it, or that, to the contrary, it did not have a sufficient impact or elicit the expected reaction.

Sadness can also be produced by some offense, or what is believed to be such: 'When we are wronged or think that we have been wronged, we become sad,' St John of Damascus observes.[1]

In nearly all these cases, and like the anger that precedes it, this passion reveals an attachment to oneself and is linked to vanity and pride. It manifests a reaction of the frustrated ego in its desire for self-affirmation (in which the second cause is joined to the first) and lowers self-esteem.[2] Often linked to sadness, rancor is also resentment for wounded pride, and anger, source of the same passion, frequently expresses a will to reaffirm, enhance, and reassure the ego vis-à-vis oneself and others. Sadness reveals itself to be then an expression of the ego's failure or impotence in its attempt at self-rehabilitation.

Unmotivated Sadness

St John Cassian tells us that 'it sometimes happens that we are suddenly filled with an anxiety that has no cause; we feel overwhelmed by a sadness for which no motive can be found.'[3] He also says that there are two different kinds of sadness: the first consists of all those varieties considered above, 'the second comes from unreasonable mental anguish or despair.'[4] The line between this kind of sadness and the passion of acedia, which we will examine below, is far from precise.

---

1. *The Orthodox Faith,* II, 16. See also St Mark the Hermit, *On Those Who Think They are Made Righteous by Works,* 180.
2. See St Barsanuphius, *Letters,* 698. St Dorotheus of Gaza, *Maxims,* 3.
3. *Conferences,* V, 11.
4. Ibid.

Demonic Activity

The demons play an important role in the birth, development and perpetuation of all the forms of sadness or depression, especially the kind just discussed. If it is said to be without cause, this is because there is no direct relationship with any definite action on the part of the person affected; because it is not, like the preceding cases, the fruit of some unsatisfied desire or of a movement of anger, but not because it truly has no cause. The Fathers recognize in such cases that it is most often produced by some demonic influence. As St John Cassian remarks,

> occasionally we are even provoked to fall into this misfortune for no apparent reason, when we are suddenly weighed down by great sorrow at the instigation of the clever foe.[1]

St John Chrysostom, in analyzing the state of his friend Stagirius who suffered from a profound depression, also stressed in several places the role of demonic influence.[2] He wrote to his friend saying:

> The devil surrounds your mind with these dark sorrows as with a deep obscurity, and strives to rob you of any thought that might reassure you. Finding your soul isolated, he overwhelms it with blows and wounds.[3]

The irruption of a sense of sadness in the soul is moreover one of the most immediate effects of demonic activity. 'The thoughts that come to one from the demon are first of all distressing and mixed with sadness,' notes St Barsanuphius.[4] Conversely, one can say that every state of sadness in the soul is in every circumstance a sign of demonic activity. 'Everything that causes distress and sadness comes from the demons,' reiterates this great elder.[5]

However external events might arise and motivate sadness, it

---

1. *The Institutes*, IX, 4. Cf. St Dorotheus of Gaza, *Instructions*, V, 67.
2. *Consolation to Stagirius*, I, 1; II, 1.
3. Ibid., II, 1.
4. *Letters*, 124. Cf. 70.
5. *Letters*, 124. Cf. 70.

must be stressed that such is truly not its real source. They are the occasion, not the cause which rather lies uniquely in the very soul of the individual, and more precisely in the attitude adopted with regard to himself and exterior events. Thus he is responsible for the sadness which affects him, both the exterior circumstances and the evils that afflict him basically only serve as excuses. St John Chrysostom tells us that

> our joys and sadness come not so much from the nature of things as from our own dispositions. If they are wisely directed we will always have a great store of contentment in our hearts. Bodily illnesses have as their cause some interior disorder rather than inclement weather or any other external influence, but this is even more so for maladies of the soul. For if those of the body are the lot of our nature, those of the soul belong only to our will.[1]

Even when the demons give rise to or maintain these states of despondency, they can do so only because they find a favorable terrain in the soul and benefit from a certain participation (more or less conscious) of the individual's will. Thus St John Chrysostom can say to Stagirius: 'The demon is not the author of this dark grief that is in you, but it is the grief itself which comes to the aid of the demon and suggests these evil thoughts.'[2] Very often sadness is prior to the direct intervention of the devil, who is only taking advantage of the situation to augment the passion.

The passion of sadness can take an extreme form, namely despair (*apognosis*).[3] This is one of its most serious manifestations. 'An excessive sadness is dangerous,' remarks St John Chrysostom, 'so dangerous that it can even cause death.'[4]

In the growth of despair the devil plays a particularly important role and by means of this condition can provoke in the soul cata-

---

1. *Homilies on the Statutes*, I, 3.
2. *Consolation to Stagirius*, II, 1. Cf. II, 13.
3. See St John Climacus, *The Ladder*, XXVI, 72. St Symeon the New Theologian, *Practical and Theological Chapters*, I, 72.
4. *Homilies on John*, LXXVIII, 1.

strophic consequences. 'The devil,' St John Chrysostom tells us, 'has no greater weapon in his hands than despair; we also give him less pleasure in sinning than in despairing.'[1] In this condition the individual basically despairs of God and cuts himself off from Him. As a result he leaves the field free for the devil's action, and, bound hand and foot, yields to his power and is given up to spiritual death. As St Paul teaches 'the sadness of the world worketh death' (2 Cor. 7:10).[2]

Under the effect of despair (and sometimes even simply from sadness), man often comes to embrace corrupt passions, thinking that they might bring a remedy for his condition, if only to save him from an awareness of this condition. Thus the Apostle states, 'having lost all hope they are free to embrace licentiousness, unto the working of all uncleanness; plunged in impurity' (Eph. 4:19). Following him St Gregory the Great tells us that the end result of sadness is 'the straying of the spirit towards forbidden things.'[3]

A source of spiritual death, despair can also lead a man to suicide: inciting him to no longer expect anything from life, it implants ideas of suicide in his soul and prompts him to accomplish them.[4] In explaining this matter St John Chrysostom maintained the possibility of a demonic influence, but stressed that it was not the only cause, as he wished to once again insist on the responsibility of the individual himself. 'These baneful thoughts' he wrote to Stagirius,

> do not only come from the demon; your own melancholy is also very much to blame. Yes indeed, this dark sadness even more than the evil spirit provokes these thoughts, and perhaps they are the only cause. It is certain that some individuals, quite apart from any demonic obsession, suffer this mania for suicide after excessive suffering.[5]

1. *Homilies on Repentance*, I, 2.
2. See St Nicetas Stethatos, *Centuries*, I, 60. St Hesychios of Batos, *On Watchfulness*, 135.
3. *Moralia on Job*, XXXI, 45.
4. One sees this in the case of Stagirius, the friend of St John Chrysostom, who was tormented with ideas of suicide and was at the point of committing the act (*Consolation to Stagirius*, I, 1 and 2; II, 1).
5. *Consolation to Stagirius*, II, 1.

He also says that

> a deep sadness, even where there is no demonic influence, gives
> birth to the greatest evils. . . . It is under the pressure of a dark
> depression that these unfortunate individuals place a noose
> around their neck, stab themselves with a dagger, try to drown
> themselves, or have recourse to other forms of violent death.
> Even those in whom the activity of the evil spirit becomes clear
> should cast less blame on it than on the tyranny and excess of
> their own grief.[1]

For all these reasons sadness is considered by the Fathers an illness of the soul;[2] one that is of great importance and with powerful
effects. *A fortiori* such is the situation with despair.[3] 'Great is the tyranny of sadness' says St John Chrysostom, 'it is an illness of the
spirit that demands considerable strength to resist it courageously
and to reject what is evil in it.'[4]

The Fathers often present this passion as a form of insanity that
manifests itself in a particularly clear manner in despair. Thus St
Syncletica, referring to the 'the sadness that comes from the enemy,'
says that it is 'full of insanity.'[5] And St John Cassian notes that,

> if through . . . fleeting and changing happenstance it has gained
> control of our soul . . . [it] weakens and oppresses (*labefatat et
> deprimit*) the mind itself . . . having destroyed all salutary coun-
> sel and driven out steadfastness of heart, [it] crazes as it were and
> stupefies the intellect, breaking and overwhelming it with a pun-
> ishing despair.[6]

The pathological effects of sadness are important and powerful.

---

1. Ibid.
2. See St John Cassian, *The Institutes*, IX, 2. St John Chrysostom, *Homilies on
the Statutes*, XVIII, 3; *Consolation to Stagirius*, III, 14. Evagrius, *On Various Evil
Thoughts*, 12, PG 79, 1158B,C. St Isaac the Syrian, *Ascetical Homilies*, 19.
3. Cf. St John Chrysostom, *Exhortations to Theodore*, I, 1.
4. *Homilies on John*, LXXVIII, 1. He also says that it is a wound, an injury to the
soul (*Homilies on the Statutes*, VI, 1).
5. *Apophthegmata*, alphabetical series, Syncletica, 27.
6. *The Institutes*, IX, 1. Cf. St John Chrysostom, *Consolation to Stagirius*, III, 13.

'Give not up thy soul to sadness and afflict not thyself in thy own counsel' observes *Ecclesiastes* (30:21). St John Chrysostom does not hesitate to say: 'a profound sadness is more harmful to us than all the attacks of the evil spirit.'[1]

Apart from the fact that sadness, if allowed to fester, almost inevitably gives rise to despair and its serious consequences, this passion produces some of the early signs of the person's passionate attitudes such as surliness,[2] wickedness,[3] rancor,[4] bitterness,[5] spite,[6] and impatience.[7] As a result this greatly disturbs the relations of the individual with his neighbors.[8]

Let us also note that like all the other passions, sadness fills the soul with darkness.[9] In the first place it clouds the mind with darkness, blinds the intelligence and considerably impairs the faculty of discernment.[10] One of its specific effects is to weigh down the soul.[11] It moreover produces in all the faculties of man a state of lethargy[12] and indifference, making him fainthearted,[13] and paralyzing his ability to act.[14] This last effect becomes particularly serious on the spiritual plane where it deprives the person of all his dynamism, thwarts his ascetic efforts, and 'pillages prayer.'[15] This is especially true when it follows upon some shortcoming.[16]

---

1. *Consolation to Stagirius*, I, 1.
2. *Consolation to Stagirius*, III, 13.
3. St Gregory the Great, *Moralia on Job*, XXXI, 45.
4. Ibid.
5. Ibid.
6. St John Cassian, *Conferences*, V, 16, St Gregory the Great, *Moralia on Job*, XXXI, 45. Not only does sadness give rise to spite, but spite is seen to increase sadness in return.
7. St John Cassian, *The Institutes*, XI, 4.
8. See St John Cassian, *The Institutes*, XI, 4.
9. St John Climacus, *The Ladder*, XXVI Summary, 18.
10. See Evagrius, *On Various Evil Thoughts*, 12.
11. St Isaac the Syrian, *Ascetical Homilies*, 68.
12. Cf. St Gregory the Great, *loc. cit.*
13. St John Cassian, *The Institutes*, IX, 11.
14. Ibid.
15. Evagrius, *Mirror of Monks*, 56. Cf. *On Various Evil Thoughts*, 11.
16. See St John Climacus, *The Ladder*, V, 33.

The Nosology of Acedia

Acedia (*akedia*) is akin to sadness,[1] and to such a degree is this the case that St Gregory the Great, the inspirer of the ascetic tradition in the West, unites the two passions of acedia and sadness into a single one.[2] The eastern ascetical tradition however distinguishes between them.[3]

The Greek term *akedia* is translated in Latin and English as *acedia*. It is actually difficult to give a translation of this term that is both simple and complete. The words 'sloth' or 'ennui' by which it is often translated only express some aspects of the complex reality that it designates.

Acedia does correspond to certain states of sloth[4] and to a state of ennui, but also involves disgust, aversion, lassitude, as well as dejection,[5] discouragement[6] apathy, torpor, nonchalance, drowsiness, somnolence,[7] and heaviness of both body[8] and soul.[9] Acedia can even induce a person to sleep[10] when he is not really tired.[11]

Acedia involves a vague and general lack of satisfaction. The person, from the moment that he is under the rule of this passion has no taste for anything. He finds everything pointless and insipid, and no longer cares about anything.[12]

Acedia thus makes a person psychically and physically unstable.[13]

1. See St John Cassian, *The Institutes*, X, 1.
2. See *Moralia on Job*, XXXI, 85, PL 76, 821.
3. Besides Evagrius and St John Cassian, see St Athanasius of Alexandria, *Life of Anthony*, XXXVI; Palladius, *Vie de S. Jean Chrysostom*, ed. Collman-Norton, p 133; St Maximus, *Centuries on Charity*, I, 67; St John Climacus, *The Ladder*, XIII.
4. Cf. St John Cassian, *Conferences*, V, 16.
5. See Hermas, *The Shepherd*, Vis. III, 19 (11) 3.
6. St Symeon the New Theologian, *Practical and Theological Chapters*, I, 66.
7. See St John Cassian, *Conferences*, V, 16.
8. See St Arsenius, *Letter*, 19. St Symeon the New Theologian, *Practical and Theological Chapters*, I, 66; 71. St John Climacus, *The Ladder*, XIII, 8.
9. See Isaac the Syrian, *Ascetical Homilies*, 68.
10. See St Symeon the New Theologian, *Practical and Theological Chapters*, I, 71. St John Cassian, *Conferences*, V, 11.
11. See St John Climacus, *The Ladder*, XIII, 12 and 8.
12. See St Diadochos of Photiki, *Hundred Chapters*, 58.
13. See St John Cassian, *The Institutes*, X, 6; *Conferences*, V, 16.

The faculties become fickle; the mind, unable to concentrate, goes from object to object. When alone, the person cannot remain in any one place; this passion forces him to leave and wander around,[1] seeking another place to live. Sometimes such a person becomes a wanderer and a vagabond.[2] In a general manner he will seek out contact with others at any price.[3] These contacts are not objectively really necessary but, under the pressure of this passion, he feels the need to contrive 'good' excuses to justify them.[4] And so he establishes and maintains these often futile relationships which he fosters with vain discussions[5] that generally betray a vain curiosity.[6]

Those afflicted with acedia often develop an intense and permanent aversion for the place where they reside.[7] Such becomes a motive for discontent and makes them believe they would be better off elsewhere.[8] They are driven 'to desire other sites where [they] can more easily procure life's necessities.'[9] Acedia can also affect their activities and especially their work which no longer gives them any sense of satisfaction.[10] This leads them to seek out other forms of employment which they think will be more interesting and make them happier...

All these situations connected with acedia are associated with a sense of unease or anxiety. Indeed, beside the sense of disgust, this is a basic mark of this passion.[11]

The demon of acedia particularly attacks those committed to the spiritual life: he seeks to turn them away from the ways of the Spirit

1. See St John Cassian, *Conferences* V, 11.
2. This can be in the imagination as well as physically. See. St John Cassian, *Conferences*, V, 16; *The Institutes*, X, 6.
3. Ibid., X, 2 (3).
4. Ibid.
5. St John Cassian, *Conferences*, V, 16.
6. Ibid.
7. See Evagrius, *Praktikos*, 12. See also *Antirrheticos*, VI, 33.
8. See St John Cassian, *The Institutes*, X, 2 (2). St Arsenius, *Letter*, 57.
9. Evagrius, *The Praktikos*, 12. Also see *Antirrheticos*, VI, 33.
10. Evagrius, Ibid.
11. St John Cassian, defines it in several places as 'tedium or anxiety of the heart' (*The Institutes*, V, I; XX, 1, *Conferences*, V, 2). See also *Conferences*, V, 16; XXIV, 5. *The Institutes*, X, 2 (3).

and to hinder their activities in various ways, undermining above all the regularity and constancy of ascetic discipline which such a life demands,[1] and interrupting the silence and stability needed to foster this life.[2] Thus St John Climacus describes this as 'a paralysis of the soul, an enervation of the mind, neglect of asceticism.'[3] It makes the spiritual person 'weak and lacking the necessary courage for the work which he must do, hindering him from persisting and applying himself to the task.'[4] Under the influence of this passion, his mind 'becomes idle and incapable of any spiritual activity,'[5] and especially experiences great difficulty when praying.[6] He becomes indifferent to 'the works of God',[7] loses all desire for future blessings,[8] and even goes so far as to disparage spiritual benefits.[9]

True, acedia especially affects those who strive to submit themselves to a regular spiritual discipline. For this reason they have limited their exterior activities and movements to what is strictly necessary, and seek the greatest possible silence and solitude. True also, the more an individual governs himself spiritually and isolates himself, devoting himself in silence to the prayer that unites one to God, the more he is attacked by this particularly dreadful passion of hermits. This passion does not, however, leave in peace those who live apart from all discipline or even any spiritual activity. As Isaac the Syrian informs us, it attacks them in other ways: 'Those who pass their life in physical works ... are assailed by another kind of despondency, one which is familiar to everyone.'[10] This acedia takes the form of an obscure and confused feeling of dissatisfaction, of

---

1. Cf. St Symeon the New Theologian, *Practical and Theological Chapters*, I: 66; 71.
2. See. St John Cassian, *The Institutes*, X, 3.
3. *The Ladder*, XIII, 2.
4. St John Cassian, *The Institutes*, X, 2 (1).
5. Ibid., (3).
6. Cf. St Arsenius, *Letter*, 19. St Isaac the Syrian, *Ascetical Homilies*, 57. St John Climacus, *The Ladder*, XIII: 3, 8, 12. St Symeon the New Theologian, *Practical and Theological Chapters*, I, 73. Cf. 66.
7. St Isaac the Syrian, *Ascetical Homilies*, 40.
8. St Diadochos of Photiki, *Hundred Chapters*, 58.
9. Ibid.
10. *Ascetical Homilies*, 50.

disgust, ennui, or listlessness vis-à-vis themselves, their life,[1] their acquaintances, the place where they live, their work, or even any activity whatsoever.[2] They are also afflicted by an irrational uneasiness and a generalized anxiety, an either episodic or continual anguish. Correlatively, they usually suffer from a state of torpor, a psychic and physical numbness, a constant and general fatigue experienced without a particular cause, and a periodic or constant somnolence of body and soul. Often, in a parallel way, in order to avert these painful states, acedia impels them to become involved in a variety of activities and to seek out non-essential changes of location or useless company; by all this they think themselves able to escape their distress and ennui, to flee solitude and quench their feelings of dissatisfaction. In this way they wish to and often believe they can satisfy and find themselves, but in reality they are running away from themselves and their spiritual obligations. They are running away from their true nature and destiny, and thus from any hope of full and complete satisfaction.

Among those leading an ascetic life, the attacks of this demon and the manifestation of this passion reach their greatest intensity around noon.

> It is especially around the sixth hour[3] [writes St John Cassian] that [this adversary] troubles [solitaries], arousing at fixed times like a fever that periodically returns, their soul-sickness by means of the distress that they kindle. Some among the ancients called this the 'noonday demon' which is spoken of in Psalm 90.[4]

Among these ancients Evagrius tells us:

---

1. Cf. St Diadochos of Photiki: 'The spirit of acedia devalorizes this temporal life,' *Hundred Chapters*, 58.
2. Cf. Abba Poemen: 'Acedia presents itself each time that one starts to do anything' (*Apophthegmata*, alphabetic series, Poemen, 157).
3. Noon. St John Climacus also points to this time of day (*The Ladder*, XIII, 5).
4. *The Institutes*, X, 1.

The demon of acedia—also called the 'noonday demon'...
presses his attack upon the monk about the fourth hour[1] and
besieges the soul until the eighth hour.[2]

What essentially distinguishes acedia from sadness is that there is
no specific motive for acedia and, as St John Cassian says 'the mind
is troubled without any reason.'[3] That there is no motive does not
mean there is no cause. As the preceding remarks indicate, a
demonic etiology is preponderant.[4] In order to act, though, it presupposes a favorable terrain. The fact that the individual is attached
to pleasure or in the grip of sadness constitutes, according to St
Thalassios, one aspect of this problem.[5] 'Acedia is an apathy of soul;
and a soul becomes apathetic when sick with self-indulgence,'[6] he
notes again. As for St Macarius, he goes further and charges a lack
of faith.[7] And St Isaac remarks that, for the spiritual person, 'acedia
is begotten of distraction of the mind.'[8]

The preceding description of the troubles associated with acedia
allows us to see why the Fathers considered it a disease of the soul.[9]
Its numerous pathological effects only confirm this way of seeing it.

Foremost among these effects is a generalized obscuring of the
soul: acedia darkens the mind (*nous*),[10] blinds it, and wraps the
entire soul in darkness.[11] As a result the soul becomes incapable of

---

1. Ten o'clock.
2. Two o'clock, *Praktikos*, 12. In chapter 36 Evagrius only uses the expression
'noonday demon' to designate acedia.
3. *The Institutes*, x, 2 (3).
4. See also St Macarius, *St Symeon Metaphrastis Paraphrase of the Homilies*, 129.
5. *Centuries*, I, 90.
6. Ibid., III, 51.
7. *St Symeon Metaphrastis Paraphrase of the Homilies*, 49.
8. *Ascetical Homilies*, 54.
9. See St John Cassian, *The Institutes*, x, 1; 2 (4); 3; f; 5; 7; 25. Evagrius, *On Various Evil Thoughts*, 12–14. St Macarius, *St Symeon Metaphrastis Paraphrase of the
Homilies*, 49. St Maximus, *Centuries on Charity*, I, 67. St Isaac the Syrian, *Ascetical
Homilies*, 42. St Thalassios, *Centuries*, III, 51.
10. St Symeon the New Theologian, *Practical and Theological Chapters*, I, 66.
11. Cf. St John Cassian, *The Institutes*, x, 2 (3), (9). St Symeon the New Theologian, *Practical and Theological Chapters*, I, 71. St Isaac the Syrian, *Ascetical Homilies*,
50.

apprehending essential truths. According to St John Cassian, 'in truth the soul which is wounded by this passion does sleep, as regards all contemplation of the virtues and insight of the spiritual senses.'[1] The most serious consequence of this passion is that the individual finds himself turned away from and kept far from the knowledge of God.[2]

Again The Fathers observe that acedia involves a laxness of soul[3] and carelessness of mind.[4] It engenders an emptiness in the soul[5] and induces a condition of generalized negligence and weakness[6] in the individual.[7] Joined to sadness, it increases it and easily leads to despair.[8] Irritability is another one of its notorious consequences.[9] In addition, according to St Isaac, 'this begets ... the spirit of aberration from which ten thousand trials gush forth.'[10]

Unlike the other principle passions, acedia does not engender any particular passion[11] because it tends to engender nearly all of them. Evagrius explains: 'The thoughts associated with acedia do not follow upon other thoughts, first of all because it is long-lasting, then because it has within it almost all the thoughts.'[12] St Maximus says much the same: 'Acedia rouses almost all the passions.'[13] St Barsanuphius tells us in a more general way that: 'The spirit of acedia begets every evil.'[14] St John Climacus notes that 'acedia is a kind of total death for the monk.'[15] And St Symeon likewise concludes that

1. *The Institutes*, X, 4.
2. See *Apophthegmata*, XI, 28.
3. St Symeon the New Theologian, *Practical and Theological Chapters*, I, 71. St John Climacus, *The Ladder*, XIII, 2.
4. St John Climacus, *The Ladder*, XIII, 2.
5. St Symeon the New Theologian, *Practical and Theological Chapters*, I, 71.
6. See ibid., 66.
7. See ibid., 72.
8. Ibid., 72.
9. St John Cassian, *Conferences*, V, 16. St Isaac the Syrian, *Ascetical Homilies*, 42.
10. *Ascetical Homilies*, 42. Cf. 32.
11. Cf. Evagrius, *Praktikos*, 12.
12. *Commentary on Psalm 139*, 3, PG 12, 1664B.
13. *Centuries on Charity*, I, 67.
14. *Letters*, 13.
15. *The Ladder*, XIII, 9.

'it is the death of mind and soul,'[1] adding 'if God allowed [this demon] to work its full power against us, no ascetic could ever be saved.'[2]

The Fathers also affirm that the totally of these effects makes acedia the most powerful and most crushing of all the passions,[3] 'the gravest of the eight deadly vices,'[4] and 'there is no passion worse than this.'[5] And St Isaac goes so far as to say that it is for the soul, 'a foretaste of Gehenna.'[6]

The treatment for acedia used by the Fathers is essentially spiritual. Let us consider various aspects of this therapy.

TREATING SADNESS

More than of any other passion, the treatment for sadness presupposes the awareness that one is ill and that one wishes to be cured. It is not unusual that, as St John Chrysostom tell us, the sickness provides the individual with certain satisfactions and 'secondary benefits'. The individual may take a morbid pleasure in his illness and passively abandon himself to this condition, sometimes without even being aware that he is the victim of this passion, a passion that is particularly serious in its unfortunate effects on the spiritual life as a whole.[7] Also St John Cassian, after having recalled these detrimental effects, writes: 'If we wish to engage in spiritual combat according to the rules, we must heal this illness with as much care as those we have previously discussed.'[8] And St John Chrysostom insists on the need for a person 'to will and desire his own healing,' and remarks that, 'to dispel sadness, it is most useful to be highly distressed by it.'[9]

1. *Practical and Theological Chapters*, I, 74.
2. Ibid.
3. St Maximus, *Centuries on Charity*, I, 67.
4. St John Climacus, *The Ladder*, XIII, 11.
5. *Apophthegmata*, alphabetical series, Poemen, 157.
6. *Ascetic Homilies*, 42.
7. *Consolation to Stagirius*, III, 14.
8. *The Institutes*, IX, 1–2.
9. *Consolation to Stagirius*, III, 14.

In the section on nosology, we have seen that sadness can have various causes. And so a specific treatment is appropriate for each case.

(a) The first possible cause of sadness is the frustration of an existing or anticipated pleasure, and more to the point the loss of some sensible good, the frustration of some desire, or disappointment over some worldly hope. With such an etiology, the treatment for sadness essentially implies the renunciation of desires and 'fleshly' pleasures, and correlatively detachment with regard to all sensible 'goods', even going so far as to hold them in contempt.[1] St Maximus remarks: 'The one who flees all the world's desires puts himself beyond every fleshly grief.'[2] And he further advises: For ... sadness disdain ... material things.'[3] St John Climacus also says

If someone has come to detest the world, he avoids sadness, but if he has an attachment to visible things then he is not as yet cleansed of sadness. For how can he avoid sadness when he is deprived of something he loves?[4]

And Evagrius tells us:

The man who flees from all worldly pleasures is an impregnable tower before the assaults of the demon of sadness. For sadness is a deprivation of sensible pleasure, whether actually present or only hoped for. And so if we continue to cherish any some affection for anything in this world it is impossible to repel this enemy, for he lays his snares and produces sadness precisely where he sees we are particularly inclined.[5]

Every passion having as its basis some carnal desire in search of some sensible pleasure, it follows that the treatment of sadness is bound up with the treatment of the other passions. Evagrius explains:

1. See St Dorotheus of Gaza, *Maxims*, 4.
2. *Centuries on Charity*, I, 22.
3. Ibid., III, 13.
4. *The Ladder*, II, 11.
5. *The Praktikos*, 19.

Sadness ensues when one does not obtain what is desired carnally. Now every passion is linked to a desire. Whoever has conquered the passions will never be dominated by sadness.... Whoever is master of his passions is master of sadness, but who is vanquished by pleasure cannot escape its bonds. Whoever loves the world will be saddened often.... But whoever disdains the pleasures of the world will not be troubled by sad thoughts.[1]

A person subject to the flesh is avid, not only for material goods, but even for honor and human glory, and we have noted in studying the passion of sadness its direct link to the passion of *cenodoxia* (vainglory). Thus disappointment in the search for honor and glory in the world is a frequent cause of sadness, as much for those who already possess them but desire more, as for those who aspire to leave their lowly state. In such cases the treatment for sadness implies contempt for this glory and for worldly honors,[2] or better still, a complete indifference in their regard, whether one benefits from them or is deprived of them. Against this aspect of sadness St Maximus counsels contempt for glory and the seeking of obscurity.[3]

(b) A second important cause of sadness is anger, whether it follows from it or is the consequence of some offence suffered, frequently taking in such a case the form of spite.

The Fathers stress the cause of sadness does not lie in those who have roused our anger and for whom we bear a grudge, nor in those who have offended us, but only in ourselves. In this instance, to sever all ties with the persons concerned would not be, then, proper therapy. Thus St John Cassian writes:

God, the Creator of all things, knowing better than anyone else how to right his handiwork and that the roots and causes of our offenses lie not in others but in ourselves, commanded that the company of the brothers should not be forsaken and that those

---

1. *On Various Evil Thoughts*, 11–12, PG 79, 1156D and 1157BC.
2. St Dorotheus of Gaza, *Maxims*, 4.
3. *Centuries on Charity*, III, 133.

persons should not be avoided who have been hurt by us or by whom we think that we have been offended.[1]

On the contrary, association with others in this situation allows for a more rapid healing than does solitude, insofar as it constitutes for the individual a test in which he directly confronts the difficulties which are the source of his sadness, and so is more easily and rapidly cured. Otherwise he runs the risks that these difficulties might become more or less unconscious while continuing to remain active and thereby keep the person immersed in sadness. On the other hand, we know that the remembrance of injuries, resentment, rancor and in general all that follows from anger, instead of spontaneously dissipating, have on the contrary a tendency to grow imperceptibly, to be reinforced under the influence of the imagination, to spread like a venom and by degrees poison the entire soul. Thus St John Cassian tells us that sadness is a component of several passions that are

> healed by a meditative heart and by constant watchfulness but also by involvement with the brothers and by their continual challenges, and when they are frequently shown to be active and are often rebuked they quite speedily find their way to health.[2]

He likewise notes that with these passions

> human companionship is of no harm, and indeed it is even of great help to those who really want to be rid of them, since they are frequently rebuked by the presence of other people, and although aggravations more readily appear, they are quickly remedied.[3]

It is from this point of view that the Fathers recommend, not only to bear no grudge against the offending person, but to see him as a benefactor, as a physician working to heal the soul, and to thank him. If one of the brothers

---

1. *The Institutes*, IX, 7.
2. Ibid., VI, 3.
3. *Conferences*, V, 4. Cf. XIX, 6.

injures or afflicts you in some way, the ancients recommend that we pray for him, as the Fathers tell us, with the thought that he is procuring great benefits for you, and that he is a physician healing you of the love of pleasure.[1]

Another counsels:

If someone retains the memory of someone who has afflicted or insulted him, he should be remembering him as a physician sent by Christ and regard him as a benefactor. For, if you are vexed under these circumstances, this is proof that your soul is sick. Indeed, if you were not sick, you would not suffer. You should then offer thanks to this brother, since thanks to him you become aware of your sickness. Pray for him and receive that which comes from him as a remedy sent by the Lord. If, on the contrary, you are vexed with him, it is as if you said to Jesus, 'I do not wish to be healed by you.'[2]

In any case it is good to pardon the offender, forsake all rancor against him, and on the contrary give him proof of your good will and charity. As St Maximus explains:

Rancor and sadness go together. When the intellect forms the image of a brother's face with a feeling of sadness, it is clear that he harbors rancor against him.[3]

If you harbor rancor against anybody, pray for him and you will prevent the passion from being aroused; for by means of prayer you will separate your resentment from the thought of the wrong he has done you. When you have become loving and compassionate towards him, you will wipe the passion completely from your soul.[4]

Rather than accuse the offender, the offended individual should accuse himself, either because he recognizes himself deserving of

1. *Apophthegmata*, xv, 135.
2. Ibid., xvi, 17.
3. *Centuries on Charity*, iii, 89.
4. Ibid., 90.

the offence because of his own sinful state, or because he acknowl-
edges having provoked the offence by some word, attitude or im-
proper action vis-à-vis the other.[1] Thus St Dorotheos of Gaza
teaches, 'If a man examines himself in the fear of God and gropes
about diligently in his own conscience, he will always find cause for
accusing himself.'[2] In every case, he explains,

> the root cause of all these disturbances [experienced as the result
> of an offense], if we are to investigate it accurately, is that we do
> not accuse ourselves; hence we have all these commotions and we
> never find rest. It is not to be wondered at that we hear from the
> holy Fathers that there is no other way but this. . . . If a man were
> to discipline himself in a thousand ways and not take this road,
> he would never stop troubling others or being troubled by them,
> and he would waste all his labors. How much joy, how much
> peace of soul would a man not have wherever he went, as Abba
> Poemen says, if he was one who habitually accused himself? For
> if anything happened to him, some punishment, a dishonor, or
> any kind of trouble, he would accept it as if he deserved it and
> would never be put to confusion. That man would have complete
> freedom from care.[3]

(c) We have seen that, apart from those forms of sadness where it
is possible to determine the precise cause, there is also an 'unmoti-
vated' sadness which can arise in the soul for no apparent reason.
For the majority of such cases this sadness is roused by a demonic
influence that is more direct than for the other ones. It is not possible in such cases to envisage a specific remedy, and a more general
approach to treatment is required, using methods similar to those
already considered in treating the other forms of sadness.

It is important that a person gripped by sadness not become
withdrawn, which would favor the advance of this illness, but be
open about his condition and disclose his thoughts to those more
spiritually advanced and speak to them about it. And so he could be

1. See St Dorotheus of Gaza, *Instructions*, VII, 82.
2. Ibid.
3. Ibid., 81.

delivered from these thoughts[1] and hear consoling words which would be an irreplaceable help for him. St John Chrysostom stresses in this way the therapeutic value of spiritual discourse for those who suffer from sadness:

> As long as the sore of sadness remains, we will apply to it the medicine of consolation. For if in the case of bodily wounds, physicians do not give over their fomentations, until they perceive that the pain has subsided; much less ought this to be done in regard to the soul. Sadness is a sore of the soul; and we must therefore foment it continually with soothing words. For not so naturally is warm water efficacious to soften a hard tumor of the flesh, as words of comfort are powerful to allay the swelling passions of the soul. Here, there is no need of the sponge as with physicians, but instead of this we employ the tongue. No need of fire here, that we may warm the water; but instead of fire, we make use of the grace of the Spirit. Suffer us then to do so to-day. For if we were not to comfort you, where else could you obtain consolation?[2]

A person so afflicted may also find needed help and consolation by reading and meditation on the appropriate passages of Holy Scripture.[3] This is a most efficacious remedy, especially if accompanied by prayer.[4]

Prayer in all its forms constitutes the chief remedy for sadness, regardless of its origin. St Nilus tells us 'Prayer is a remedy for sadness and for depression.'[5]

Although psalmody is proven to be a particularly efficacious mode of prayer against the kind of sadness that comes directly from demons,[6] the prayer of the heart practiced with watchfulness and attention appears to be the preeminent remedy for all forms of sad-

---

1. Cf. St Hesychios of Batos, *On Watchfulness*, 136.
2. *Homilies on the Statutes*, VI, 1.
3. Cf. Evagrius, *Antirrheticos*, Sadness.
4. Cf. St John Chrysostom, *Consolation to Stagirius*, III, 14.
5. *Apophthegmata*, alphabetical series, Nilus, 3. Cf. Evagrius, *Chapters on Prayer*, 16. St Hesychios of Batos, *On Watchfulness*, 135.
6. See *Apophthegmata*, alphabetical series, Syncletica, 21.

ness. St John Cassian, who notes that sadness is one of the passions which are 'healed by a meditative heart and by constant watchfulness,'[1] later states:

> We shall, therefore, be able to expel this most pernicious passion from ourselves once our mind is occupied constantly with spiritual meditation. . . . For we shall be able to overcome every kind of sadness—whether that which derives from previous anger, or that which befalls us when a loss of money or some other disadvantage strikes us, or that which occurs when some injury has been inflicted on us, or that which proceeds from an irrational turn of mind, or that which brings upon us a deadly despair.[2]

Treating Acedia

We have seen in describing the passion of acedia that it has the peculiarity of seizing all the faculties of the soul and inflaming nearly all the passions. St John Climacus tells us that 'acedia is a kind of total death.'[3] As St John Cassian stresses, this particular quality requires a manifold therapy: anyone

> who wishes to engage lawfully in the struggle for perfection, must . . . contend on both sides against this most wicked spirit of acedia.[4]

Treatment supposes that the illness has been brought to light and recognized as such, for this passion is notable for having no apparent cause and hence for being unconscious or incomprehensible. This is particularly the case because one of its principal effects is to blind the mind and to render the entire soul confused. This is why St John Cassian writes that whoever wishes to combat it 'must strive to cast out this disease as well from the depths of his soul.'[5] And

1. *The Institutes*, VI, 3.
2. Ibid., IX, 13.
3. *The Ladder*, XIII, 9.
4. *The Institutes*, X, 5.
5. Ibid.

Abba Poemen on his part notes that 'if a man recognizes it for what it is, he will gain peace.'[1]

This passion being characterized, especially among solitaries, by the need to quit one's cell and go about seeking contact with others, it must first of all be recognized that the individual's justifications for this need are nothing more than a vain pretext dictated by the passion itself. This will help him avoid giving in to these so-called needs. The Fathers unanimously recommend that, when this passion occurs under this form, the person struggle to resist it by first of all striving not to leave the place where he finds himself under any pretext whatsoever.

> The time of temptation [writes Evagrius] is not the time to leave one's cell, devising plausible pretexts. Rather, stand there firmly and be patient. Bravely take all that the demon brings upon you, but above all face up to the demon of acedia.[2]

And again he advises: 'When the spirit of acedia arises in you, do not quit the house or evade the struggle.'[3] St John Cassian similarly advises that one must fight against the spirit of acedia so that one is not 'driven out from the bulwark of the monastery and depart in flight, even for a seemingly pious reason.'[4]

When acedia manifests a tendency towards sleepiness, it is also good to resist it by forcing oneself not to give in to torpor or sleep.[5] In every case, St John Cassian remarks, 'experience proves that an onslaught of acedia must not be avoided by flight but overcome by resistance.'[6]

To give in to acedia is in any case a bad solution that will only intensify the illness. As St John Cassian notes:

> The unhappy soul, preyed upon by devices like these of the enemy, is agitated until, worn out by the spirit of acedia...

---

1. *Apophthegmata*, alphabetical series, Poemen, 149.
2. *The Praktikos*, 28.
3. *Sentences for Monks*, 55, ed. Gressmann, p157.
4. *The Institutes*, x, 5. See also St Isaac the Syrian, *Ascetical Homilies*, 50.
5. See St John Cassian, *The Institutes*, x, 3; 5.
6. Ibid., x, 25.

either learns to succumb to sleep or shakes off the restraints of the cell and gets in the habit of finding its consolation in the face of this onslaught by visiting a brother, although it will be all the more painfully vulnerable not long after.... The adversary will the more frequently and harshly try a person who he knows, once the battle is joined, will immediately offer him his back and who he sees hopes for safety not in victory or in struggle but in flight.[1]

And elsewhere he says the same about those attacked by acedia:

If ... they concede themselves the freedom of going out often, they will bring a worse plague upon themselves by this remedy, as they think it is. It is the same with certain people who believe that they can quell the force of internal fevers with a drink of very cold water, when in fact it is clear that this stirs up the fire rather than settling it, since a far graver sickness follows the momentary relief.[2]

Just as the cause of acedia lies within the individual and not in his solitary condition, so also the principle way to heal this malady is to seek its source in the relationship of an individual with himself and not with others. The sense of being able to receive help from others is in the majority of cases fallacious. St Isaac the Syrian writes with regard to this:

The healing of these [trials of acedia] wells up from *hesychia*[3] itself. This is the man's consolation. But he will never receive the light of consolation from intercourse with men, and their converse will never heal him, but only briefly give him rest; thereafter these trials will rise up against him with great force.... Blessed is he who patiently endures these things within the doors [of his cell].[4]

---

1. Ibid., X, 3.
2. *Conferences*, XXIV, 5.
3. Recall that the Greek word *esukhia* signifies a state of silence, calmness (exterior and interior), and solitude.
4. *Ascetical Homilies*, 50.

The Fathers acknowledge that sometimes 'of necessity he must have a man who is enlightened and has experience in these matters, so that by him he can be enlightened and strengthened at the time of his need.'[1] But this can only be the exception rather than the rule.[2]

However, resistance to this passion never provides immediate results. Almost always victory over acedia supposes a long and diligent struggle.[3] Also and above all treatment demands that one give proof of patience and perseverance. The virtue of patience appears to be one of the chief remedies of this passion.[4] Evagrius tells us that 'acedia is quelled by patience (*upomone*).'[5] And St Maximus stresses that this treatment was given to us by Christ himself:

Acedia alone seizes control of all the soul's powers and rouses almost all the passions together. That is why this passion is more serious than all the others. Hence our Lord has given us an excellent remedy against it, saying: 'You will gain possession of your souls through your patient endurance' (Luke 21:19).[6]

Hope is as if another fundamental remedy and it should be joined to patience.[7] The hopeful man, as St John Climacus teaches, 'slays acedia, kills it with his sword.'[8] And Evagrius counsels:

When we meet the demon of acedia... we are to sow the seeds of a firm hope in ourselves while we sing with the holy David: 'Why are you filled with sadness, my soul? Why are you distraught?

---

1. St Isaac the Syrian, *Ascetical Homilies*, 50. Cf. St Basil the Great, *Monastic Rules*, VII, 2, PG 31, 1368A.

2. Cf. Isaac the Syrian, *Ascetical Homilies*, 50.

3. Ibid.

4. See St Macarius, *St Symeon Metaphrastis Paraphrase of the Homilies*, 129. St John Climacus, *The Ladder*, XXVII, 84. St Barsanuphius, *Letters*, 13. St Dorotheus of Gaza, *Instructions*, XII, 133.

5. *Sentences for Monks*, PG 79 1236A. Cf. *Praktikos*, 28.

6. *Centuries on Charity*, I, 67.

7. Cf. *St Symeon Metaphrastis Paraphrase of the Homilies*, 129. St John Climacus, *The Ladder*, XXVII, 84.

8. *The Ladder*, XXX, 34.

Hope in God for I shall give praise to him. He it is who saves me, the light of my eyes and my God' (Ps. 42:6).[1]

The hope that one has is not only for a more or less long term deliverance from this passion and the obtaining of peace,[2] but also for future blessings which St John Climacus says constitutes a judgment over this passion[3] and its utter annihilation.[4]

A third essential remedy is repentance, sorrow and compunction. One of the ancients taught that if the individual 'keeps his sins in mind, God will be his help in everything and he will not suffer from acedia.'[5] St John Climacus counsels that 'this tyrant should be overcome by the remembrance of past sins.'[6] And he also says that whoever 'mourns for himself does not suffer from acedia.'[7] The tears which accompany repentance and spiritual sorrow appear to be an even more powerful remedy. Evagrius tells us that 'acedia is suppressed by tears,'[8] and adds that 'to shed tears is a great remedy for the night visions engendered by acedia. This is the remedy that David wisely applied to his own passions, saying 'I have toiled in my groaning; every night I will wash my bed, with tears will I water my couch' (Ps. 6:6).[9]

The 'remembrance of death' (*mneme thanatou*)[10] is another important remedy. This fundamental ascetic practice consists of the individual continually remembering that he is mortal and might die at any moment. To this 'remembrance of death' is attached the counsel often formulated by the Fathers that one should 'live as if

1. *The Praktikos*, 27. Evagrius counsels the same treatment and quotes the same passage from Scripture in *Antirrheticos*, VI, 20.
2. See *Apophthegmata*, XXI, 7.
3. *The Ladder*, XIII, 7.
4. Ibid.
5. *Apophthegmata*, PA 32, 7c.
6. *The Ladder*, XIII, 15.
7. Ibid., XIII, 15. Cf. XXVII, 84.
8. *Mirror of Virgins*, 39, ed. Gressmann, p149. Cf. *The Praktikos*, 27.
9. *Antirrheticos*, VI, 10, ed. Frankenberg, p522, 32–35. Cf. Ibid., 19, p524, 22; 'Souls may think that tears serve no purpose in the struggle against acedia, but they forget that this is just what David was doing when he said: "My tears have become my bread day and night" (Ps. 41:4).'
10. See St John Climacus, *The Ladder*, XIII, 16.

each day was one's last', a counsel which is not so much about pre-paring a man to die well as to live well. The 'remembrance of death' has as its principle purpose to help man not squander the precious time given to him for the saving of his soul; to allow him in the words of St Paul, to 'redeem the time' (Eph. 5:16), and so to live each moment with maximum spiritual intensity, avoid sin, practice the commandments, and give himself totally to God. The 'remem-brance of death' is particularly effective in cases of acedia, insofar as acedia is a state of indifference, lethargy, and spiritual laziness, makes the individual negligent with regard to his salvation, and impels him into some activity, a change of place, or futile relation-ships which are, from the spiritual point of view, a diversion and a waste of time. One of the *Apophthegmata* tells us: 'One of the old men was asked why he was never discouraged? And he replied: "Because every day I expect to die."'[1] And St Anthony the Great teaches:

> To avoid being heedless, it is good to consider the word of the Apostle, 'I die daily' (1 Cor. 15:31). For if we too live as though dying daily, we shall not sin. And the meaning of that saying is, that as we rise day by day we should think that we shall not abide till evening; and again, when about to lie down to sleep, we should think that we shall not rise up.[2]

Evagrius counsels us in his *Antirheticos* to counter thoughts of ace-dia with these verses taken from the Scriptures: 'Man's days are as grass, as the flower of the field so shall he flourish. For the spirit shall pass in him, and he shall not be: and he shall know his place no more' (Ps. 102:15–16).[3] And 'Our life on earth passes like a shadow' (Job 8:9); 'our existence only lasts a few days' (Job 10:20).[4] And he recalls the teaching of his spiritual father on this subject:

> Our holy and most ascetic master stated that the monk should always live as if he were to die on the morrow.... For [by this

1. *Apophthegmata*, XXI, 7.
2. *Life of Anthony*, 19.
3. *Antirrheticos*, VI, 25.
4. Ibid., 32 and 33.

attitude] he will be able to cut off every thought that comes from acedia and thus become more fervent.[1]

This attitude is justified by the preceding consideration, but also by the fact that, as Evagrius notes elsewhere, the demon of acedia 'depicts life stretching out for a long period of time,'[2] seeking by this to inspire in him a slackness about and a distaste for future difficulties, especially for 'the toil of the ascetic struggle.'[3]

The fear of God is another powerful antidote to this passion. According to St John Climacus, 'nothing else is quite so effective.'[4]

Manual labor is also among the remedies prescribed by the Fathers.[5] It helps the individual avoid the boredom, instability, torpor, and sleepiness that together form one aspect of this passion. It can contribute to establishing and maintaining diligence, the continual presence of mind, effort, and attention implied by the spiritual life and which acedia seeks to disrupt. Above all it is directly opposed to indolence, one of the principle forms assumed by acedia and the source of innumerable evils. St John Cassian, while referring to the teaching of St Paul, gives a lengthy presentation of manual labor as a remedy for acedia which he envisages under this last form.

The blessed Apostle [he writes] already saw this malady, which springs from the spirit of acedia, creeping in, or else he foresaw, thanks to a revelation of the Holy Spirit, that it would arise, and he hastens to head it off with the health-giving remedies of his precepts. For in writing to the Thessalonians he first, like a very skilled and accomplished physician, applies the mild and soothing lotion of his words to his patients' diseased place and, beginning with love, praises them in that regard, until the deadly wound, soothed with gentler medication, can more easily sustain harsher remedies, once the angry swelling has gone down.[6]

1. *The Praktikos*, 29.
2. Ibid. 12.
3. Ibid.
4. *The Ladder*, XXVII, 75.
5. See St John Climacus, *The Ladder*, XIII, 16. St John Cassian, *The Institutes*, X, 7–24.
6. *The Institutes*, X, 7.

After having stressed the Apostle's therapeutic approach, St John lists the guidelines for the proposed remedy: 1) 'make an effort to be quiet'(1 Thess. 4:11). This means, he comments, 'as you stay in your cells, you are not to be disquieted by the different rumors...; 2) 'pursue your own affairs' (1 Thess. 4:11), which is to say 'you must not wish, out of curiosity, to inquire into the deeds of the world or wish, while looking into other people's ways of life, to expend your efforts not on your own improvement and on the pursuit of virtue but rather on calumniating your brothers'; 3) 'work with your own hands as we commanded you' (1 Thess. 4:11). Next St John recalls and comments[1] on the example that St Paul makes of his own conduct in the second letter to the Thessalonians:

> For you yourselves know how you should imitate us, for we were not disorderly among you . . . we worked night and day in labor and weariness, so as not to be a burden to any of you. (2 Thess. 3:7–8)

And after quoting the rest of this passage where St Paul mentions those 'walking in disquietude, not working but acting as busybodies (2 Thess. 3:11), St John remarks that the Apostle

> hastens to apply the appropriate remedy . . . [and] reverts once more to the compassionate attitude of a . . . kind physician, and by his healthful counsel he offers salutary medication . . . saying: 'We charge those who are such and beseech them in the Lord Jesus to work in silence and to eat their own bread' (2 *Thess.* 3:12). Like the most skilled physician, with a single healthful precept about work he has cured the causes of so many hurts that spring from the root of idleness, knowing that other maladies, too, that rise from the same soil will be destroyed as soon as the source of the initial disease has been removed.[2]

At the same time he stresses the therapeutic value of St Paul's counsels relative to manual labor. St John also indicates their prophylactic value:

1. Ibid., 7–9.
2. Ibid., 14.

Yet, like a very far-sighted and prudent physician, he not only wishes to cure the ailments of the sick but also ... offers appropriate precepts to the well whereby their health can be lastingly maintained.[1]

In closing his discussion on this point, St John cites the example of the Abba Paul who, even though he lived in a place far removed from any city where he could sell the products of his labor, nevertheless imposed on himself a certain amount of daily work 'and when his cave was filled with a whole year's work, he would burn up what he had so carefully toiled over each year.' And he concludes: 'to that extent proving that without manual labor a monk can neither stay in one spot nor ever mount to the summit of perfection.' He worked not because he had to do so to eat, but 'just for the sake of purging his heart, firming his thoughts, persevering in his cell, and conquering and driving out acedia.'[2]

Lastly, prayer is the most fundamental of all remedies for acedia,[3] for the individual cannot be delivered from this passion apart from the grace of God, and this he cannot receive without asking for it by prayer. Without this latter remedy, all the others would only be partially successful; it is from prayer that they in fact derive all their power. This is why the struggle against the passions, one's resistance in opposing them, the patience exhibited, the hope manifested, the grief and the tears, the remembrance of death, and manual labor should always be accompanied by prayer which establishes them in God and makes of them not just simply human means.

There is a problem however in the fact that acedia induces a person to abandon prayer and hinders him from having recourse to it. It is essential then that he resist this temptation with all his strength and safeguard prayer if he has not as yet abandoned it, or struggle to regain it if he has already given it up. The simultaneous practice of

1. Ibid., 15.
2. Ibid., 24. On the general significance of manual labor within the framework of an ascetic life, read the study of A. Guillaumont, *Aux origines du monachisme chrétien*, Bellefontaine, 1979, chap. VII 'Le Travail manuel dans le monachisme ancien. Conestation et valorization', pp 117–126.
3. See Evagrius, *Chapters on Prayer*, 16. St John Climacus, *The Ladder*, XIII, 116.

prostrations is especially recommended in the case of acedia because it compels the body to directly participate in prayer, for the body is subject to the same torpor as the soul and contributes to drawing both into a state of lethargy. St Symeon the New Theologian recommends:

> Since you know the cause and origin of these things that come upon you, you must make every effort to go into your usual place of prayer and prostrate yourself before God, the lover of man. Pray to him with sighs and tears in the affliction of your heart, [and ask him] to deliver you from the heaviness of acedia and these wicked thoughts. If you strike hard and with perseverance, deliverance from these things will soon be given.[1]

Psalmody seems to be a form of prayer which is particularly efficacious against acedia,[2] as is the prayer of the heart practiced with vigilance and concentration, as stressed by St Diadochos of Photiki:

> To avoid this passion which dejects and enervates us, we must confine the mind within very narrow limits, devoting ourselves solely to the remembrance of God. Only in this way will the intellect be able to regain its original fervor and escape this senseless dissipation.[3]

Because acedia in a certain manner contains within itself all the other passions, no passion will appear immediately after it is destroyed. 'No other demon follows close upon the heels of this one but only a state of deep peace . . . arises out of this struggle,' notes Evagrius. [4]

Apart from this repose, the chief effect of victory over this passion is an 'inexpressible joy' which fills the soul.[5]

With these the two examples of sadness and acedia we clearly see

---

1. *Practical and Theological Chapters*, I, 60.
2. See St John Climacus, *The Ladder*, XIII, 16.
3. *Hundred Chapters*, 58.
4. See Evagrius, *The Praktikos*, 12. St Isaac the Syrian, *Ascetical Homilies*, 46. St Hesychios of Batos, *On Watchfulness and Holiness*, 136.
5. See Evagrius, *The Praktikos*, 12.

how the psychic is integrated into the spiritual plane, and is dependent on it for both etiology and treatment. But we also see how the spiritual dimension exceeds and transcends the psychic dimension.

5

A MOST SINGULAR
KIND OF FOLLY—
THE FOOL FOR CHRIST

EASTERN CHRISTIANITY RECOGNIZES a number of saints that are venerated as 'fools for Christ'.

Among these the most celebrated during the Byzantine period to which our study is limited are:

St Ammonas,[1] the first one to be recognized, who lived in the Egyptian desert in the fourth century; St Isidora († about 365), who resided as a cloistered nun in the convent of Tabennesiotes, known of from Palladius's *Lausiac History*;[2] an anonymous monk[3] living at the beginning of the fifth century in the community of Abba Silvanus located in the southern part of Judea; certain 'grazing' monks spoken of by Evagrius the Scholastic in his *Ecclesiastical History*;[4] St. Mark the Fool[5] (fifth-sixth century) who lived in Alexandria; Theophilus and Maria[6] who lived in Amida in the sixth century; Priscus,

---

1. *Apophthegmata*, alphabetical series, Ammnas 9, PG 65, 121C.

2. Chap. XXXIV The name Isidora comes from the long recension in the *Lausiac History* (PG 34, 1101–1107).

3. Source: John Rufus, *Plérophories,* ed. F. Nau, *Patrologia Orientalis,* t. VIII, pp 178–179.

4. I, 21, ed. Bidez-Parmentier, pp 30–33.

5. Source: *Vie de Daniel le Scétiote,* ed. of the Greek text by L. Clugnet, *Review de l'Orient chrétien,* 5, 1900, chap. III, pp 60–62.

6. Source: John of Amida (also known as John of Ephesus), *Lives of the Eastern Saints.* Syriac text edited with English translation by E. W. Brooks, *Patrologia Orientalis,* t. XIX, 1926, chap. LII, Life of Theophilus and Maria, pp 164–179.

known to John of Amida[1] during his stay in Constantinople (sixth century); Antiochus or John the Sabaite who we know of from *The Ladder* of St John Climacus;[2] St Symeon,[3] unquestionably the best known of all because the first for whom a complete life was written, who lived in Emesa in the sixth century; St Andrew of Constantinople,[4] who lived in the ninth century and whose *Life* was as widely read as Symeon of Emesa's; Basil the Younger[5] who lived in Constantinople in the tenth century; Hierotheus[6] who was a monk in the monastery (*laura*) of Symeon the New Theologian (eleventh century); St Cyril the Phileote,[7] who was a contemporary of Hierotheus; St Sabbas the Younger (†1348),[8] and St Maximus the Kausokalybite[9] (fourteenth century).

1. John of Amida, *Lives of the Eastern Saints*, t. XIX, chap. LIII, Life of Priscus, pp179–185.

2. IV, 121.

3. Léontios de Neapolis, *Vie de Syméon le Fou*, ed. with commentary by A.–J. Festugière, Paris, 1974. [For the English translation see Derek Krueger, *Symeon the holy fool: Leontius's Life and the late antique city*, (Berkeley: University of California Press, 1996).]

4. Nicephorus, *Life of Andrew Saloi*, PG 111, 628C–888D. See J. Grosdidier de Matons, 'Les themes d'edification dans la Vie d'Andre Salos,' *Travaux et mémoires du Centre de recherche d'histoire et de civilisation Byzantines*, IV, Paris, 1970, pp277–328.

5. Sources: BHG (3), 264.

6. Nicetas Stethatos, *Vie de Syméon le Nouveau Théologien*, ed. I. Hausherr, chaps. LII-LVII.

7. *Vie de S. Cyrille le Philéote*, ed. and trans. by E. Sargologos, 'Subsidia Hagiographica', no. 39, Bruxelles, 1964.

8. Sources: Papadopoulos-Kerameus, *Analekia Ierosolumitikes Stakhuologias*, V, Saint-Petersbourg, 1898, pp190–359. Cf. A.-J. Festugière, 'Etude sur la Vie de S. Sabbas le Jeune qui simulait la folie', in Léontios de Néapolis, *Vie de Syméon le Fou*, pp223–249.

9. Sources: *Deux vies de St Maximus le Kausokalybite, ermite au Mont Athos*, XIVᵉ, ed. F. Halkin, *Analecta Bollandiana*, 54, 1936, pp38–112. We have not listed the person cited by St John Moschus in chapter 111 of *The Spiritual Meadow* who does not seem to be a true fool for Christ, nor St Serapion the Sindonite (*Lausiac History*, XXXVII) who intended to take off his clothes in public with complete impassibility, but did not do it and betrayed no other mark of folly. Nor do we include St Symeon the Studite. The reasoning of I. Rosenthal-Kamarinea ('Symeon Studites, ein hl. Narr', *Akten des internationale Byuzantinistenkongresses München*, 1959, Munich, 1960, pp515–520) does not seem to be at all convincing.

The phenomena of insanity assumed for the sake of Christ is sufficiently strange and intriguing for it to already be the focus of several studies,[1] but these studies have never properly interpreted the subject which remains poorly understood. Because of traits in common, the Fool for Christ is often confused with similar ascetic types, so in what follows we will both draw out its deep significance and distinguish its salient features.

THE FOOL FOR CHRIST, THE ILLITERATE, THE SIMPLE, AND THE INNOCENT

The Fool for Christ is sometimes confused with the illiterate.[2] We know that in *Acts*, Peter and John were characterized as 'men without learning and ignorant' (4:13) and many of the Fathers lay claim to such a spiritual quality.[3] This valorization however stems less from an opposition between worldly wisdom and divine folly than from the incompatibility between God's wisdom and the world's.

---

1. For the Byzantine period see E. Benz, 'Heilige Narrheit', Kyrio, 3, 1938, pp1–55. T. Spidlik, 'Fous pour le Christ en Orient': *Dictionnaire de spiritualité*, t. V, 1964, col. 752-758. A.–J. Festugière, Introduction to Léontios de Néapolis, *Vie de Syméon le Fou*, Paris, 1974, pp1–30. J. Grosdidier de Matons, 'Les thèmes d'édification dans la Vie d'André Salos', *Travaux et mémoires du Centre de recherche d'histoire et de civilisation Byzantines*, IV, Paris, 1970, pp277–328. H. Petzold, 'Zur Frömmigkeit der heiligen Narren', in *Die Einheit der Kirche, Festgabe P. Meinhold*, Wiesbaden, 1977, pp140–153. L. Ryden, 'The Holy Fool', in *The Byzantine Saint*, S. Hackel (ed.), *Studies supplementary to Sobornost*, 5, London, 1981, pp106–113. J. Saward, *Perfect Fools: Folly for Christ's Sake in Catholic and Orthodox Spirituality*, New York, 1980. With regard to cases in Russia consult the excellent studies of E. Behr-Sigel, 'Les Fous pour le Christ et la sainteté laïque dans l'ancienne Russie', *Irénikon*, 15, 1938, pp554–564, reprinted in *Prière et sainteté dans l'Église russe*, Paris, 1950, pp92–103. I. Kologrivof, *Essai sur la sainteté en Russie*, Paris, 1953. V. Rochcau, 'Que savons-nous des fous pour le Christ?', *Irénikon*, 1980, pp341–353, 501–512.

2. See T. Spidlik, 'Fous pour le Christ', op. cit., col. 755.

3. See *Apophthegmata*, alphabetical series, Arsenius, 6. St Justin, *First Apology*, 60. St Athanasius of Alexandria, *Life of Anthony*, LXXII–LXXIII. St John Cassian, *Conferences*, I, 2. St Maximus the Confessor, *Letters*, 19, PG 91, 593D. *Opuscules théologiques et polémiques*, 10, PG 91, 133B; 229B. St Nicetas Stethatos, *Life of St Symeon the New Theologian*, 135.

God destroys the wisdom of the wise and the prudence of the prudent (1 Cor. 1:19) which is a pseudo-knowledge,[1] in order to bestow by the Holy Spirit true knowledge on those who are worthy, not because of the intellectual aptitudes, but because of their level of purity and virtue acquired in the practice of the commandments. From this point of view, every Christian ascetic can lay claim to such an ignorance, which should not be considered as proper to fools for Christ, who do not moreover bring this up when speaking of themselves, their 'folly' sufficiently disqualifying them with respect to the wisdom and knowledge of this world.

Neither should the fools for Christ be compared to the 'simple', several instances of whom occur in Eastern hagiography,[2] but who have almost nothing in common with those popularly referred to as the 'simple-minded'. Their simplicity is to a great extent similar to that 'poverty of spirit' spoken of in the Beatitudes (Matt. 57:3), which in the spirituality of Eastern Christianity is considered a virtue opposed to the abundance of thoughts (*logismoi*) that act as an obstacle to interior purity and undistracted prayer. This simplicity is also opposed to all forms of self-attachment and thus seems to be quite straight-forwardly linked to another virtue, namely monastic obedience.[3] It is the fruit of an ascetic process that the Greek Fathers call *aplosis* (simplification) and which is at once renunciation, purification, and unification.[4] Although the Fool for Christ is, in this sense, a simpleton, the simpleton is not a fool; the simpleton's behavior is in every way perfectly sensible and recognized to be such.

---

1. See 1 Tim. 6:20, Evagrius, *Sentences for Monks*, 43. St Isaac the Syrian, *Letters*, 4. St Symeon the New Theologian, *Theological Discourses*, I, 271 seq.; *Ethical Discourses*, I, 184–185 and IX, 105–106. St Gregory Palamas, *Triads*, I, 1, 2, and 12.

2. One of the most famous among them was Paul the Simple, a disciple of St Anthony (see Palladius, *Lausiac History*, XXII. *History of the Monks of Egypt*, XXIV. *Apophthegmata*, alphabetical series, Paul the Simple).

3. This link is clearly seen in the *Lives* of Paul the Simple.

4. St Anthony seems to see a close relationship between the simplicity of Paul the Simple and his spiritual perfection: 'Anthony [was] convinced . . . that Paul had a perfect soul, being very simple and grace co-operating with him" (Palladius, *Lausiac History*, XXII, 9).

Fools for Christ were also confused with those 'innocents' who correspond on the one hand to the 'simple-minded', as we usually understand the term, and who often became the object of popular veneration among Eastern Christians. Dostoyevsky's novel *The Idiot* extols such an ideal figure in the person of Prince Myshkin.

In a first sense, these innocents or 'simple-minded' are human beings whose intellectual capabilities are limited due either to a handicap of biological origin or to an educational deficiency in early childhood. They correspond to what modern psychology terms mild or moderate mental deficiency.

In a second sense, they are individuals typically represented by 'the idiot' in Dostoyevsky's novel, people little acquainted with worldly conventions and ignorant of any psychological complication in dealing with others, as well as of any complication in their intellectual outlook. Hence they have a frankness hardly welcome among the hypocrisies of polite society, and a certain awkwardness in the way they behave and relate to others which makes them seem like oafs to be laughed at. On the other hand, compensating for their limited rational capacity, they seem to have an intuitive faculty which makes their judgments especially insightful and are sometimes capable of surprising foresight.

Fools for Christ do not correspond to either one or the other of these two types of innocents.

Not only do they not suffer any intellectual handicap, but in reality, as we shall see, they possess a superlative ability to feign their state of insanity, to perfectly adapt it to the situations they encounter and the spiritual goals they wish to achieve, giving symbolic significance to their acts and their words, and concealing the good they do. At the same time, they knowingly practice a social ineptitude, while many of the innocents that modern psychopathology labels 'mildly retarded' manifest a remarkable ability to adapt to their environment, showing themselves to be 'docile, hard workers, methodical, desirous of doing well, passive and obedient.'[1]

On the other hand, although the innocent of the Dostoyevskian type is oafish and clumsy from being too simple and direct, he does

1. H. Ey, P. Bernard, C. Brisset, op. cit., p 634.

not evince any behavior that is really pathological from the psychiatric point of view, while the 'fool for Christ', from this same point
of view, by his incoherent speech and disorderly actions, or, to the
contrary, by his mutism, exhibits symptoms characteristic of real
insanity. We are told that St Mark of Alexandria 'twirled like a fool
and raved.'[1] The monk of Abba Silvanus would burst out laughing
for no reason whenever he met anyone.[2] José Grosdidier de Matons
rightly comments with regard to St Symeon:

> What especially strikes us in reading [his] *Life* is the plausibility
> and coherence with which the saint sustains his role as fool: one
> psychiatrist, who had been given his *Life* to read, easily recog-
> nized a quite typical case of mania. . . . We recognize the maniac
> in all [his] deeds and gestures: in his incoherent speech, his
> excessive familiarity, his eccentric taste in clothing, his unkempt
> appearance which sometimes bordered on exhibitionism, and
> above all his fits of temper and violence that he engages in when
> upset or when someone objects to what are considered his
> caprices.[3]

On the other hand, with Cyril the Phileote and St Sabbas the Younger,
we find a mutism characteristic of certain forms of psychosis.

A SIMULATED FOLLY

All the same, and here we have another important distinction, the
fool for Christ is not really insane; he is even completely sound of
mind.[4] He pretends to be a fool, has chosen to appear the fool, and
does everything he can to seem to be so in the eyes of others, so that
he is really believed to be a fool. He controls every act and word,
precisely calculating their effect. For certain individuals who have

---

1. *Vie de Marc le Fou*, p 60.
2. John Rufus, *Plerophories*, p 178.
3. 'Les Thèmes d'édification dans la Vie d'André Salos", pp 302–303.
4. See St Isaac the Syrian, *Ascetical Homilies*, 6. *Vie de S. Sabbas le Jeune*, pp 221–
222.

discovered his secret or he himself has chosen, he lays aside this mask of foolishness, just as he does whenever he is alone, and reveals himself to be perfectly sound of mind. When foolishness for Christ is only a temporary episode in his life, both before and after his behavior shows no pathological traits. A real fool, while always having the possibility of taking folly for Christ upon himself, can not be a fool for Christ in the traditional sense. Folly in this later case is not imposed, he imposes it on himself. It is a situation that he has chosen—he can lay aside whenever he wishes or take up again whenever he deems it useful. It is not for him a handicap and in no way disturbs his psychic life, nor troubles or impedes his spiritual life.[1] He is like an actor who totally invests himself in his role, but nevertheless remains himself.

The fact that the folly of the fool for Christ is simulated is stressed by all the hagiographic texts. It is said of Ammonas that he 'feigned madness (emoropoiei).'[2] Abba Or counselled this practice: 'If you are fleeing, flee from men; or the world and the men in it will make you do many foolish things.'[3] The tale concerning Isidora is entitled 'The Nun Who Feigned Madness' (peri tes upokrinomenes morian) and begins in this way: 'In this monastery [of Tabennesiot] there was another virgin who feigned madness (upokrinomenes morian).'[4] The monk of Abbot Silvanus is said to have 'played he fool', to have 'pretended to be a fool.'[5] St Mark of Alexandria is precise:

this brother pretended to be a fool (prospoioumenos eauton salon)[6] and told us himself how it was that he adopted this manner of living: 'I said to myself: Now go to the village and make like a fool (poieson eauton salon).[7]

John of Ephesus tells us of Theophilus and Maria, who 'used constantly to perform drolleries and buffooneries,' with she dressing as

---

1. See Life of Symeon the Fool, p159.
2. Apophthegmata, alphabetical series, Ammonas, 9.
3. Ibid., Or, 14; PG 65, 440C.
4. Lausiac History, XXXIV, 1.
5. John Rufus, Plerophories, p178, 1, 10, and 29.
6. Vie de Marc le Fou, p60, 1, 10–11.
7. Ibid., p61, I. 14.

a courtesan and he as a mime; they assumed this mode of dress to 'deceive the spectators'.[1] The biography of Symeon affirms in many ways the deceptive character of his folly,[2] especially when we read:

> He played all sorts of roles foolish and indecent. . . . Sometimes he pretended to have a limp, sometimes he jumped around, sometimes he dragged himself along on his buttocks, sometimes he stuck out his foot for someone running and tripped him. Other times when there was a new moon, he looked at the sky and fell down and thrashed about. Sometimes also he pretended to babble, for he said that of all the semblances, this is most fitting and most useful to those who simulate folly.[3]

But the same source notes that when he found himself alone with his friend John, 'the old man did not act like a fool at all,' so much was this the case that according to the latter: 'I almost doubted that he had been a fool only moments before.'[4] Nicetas Stethatos notes that Hierotheus *'often had the look of intending* to turn the vases he carried upside down, or even to break them,'[5] and that his spiritual father 'was fully aware of the stratagems of Hierotheus.'[6] It is said of St Cyril the Phileote that 'the saint sometimes had the custom of playing the fool (*moropoiein*) according to God.'[7] St Sabbas the Younger is also presented as someone 'playing the fool (*ton moron upokrimenos*),' or 'feigning in appearance an insane person (*morian dethen upokrimenos*).'[8]

It is difficult for us to understand what motivates a person to simulate insanity, whether momentarily or for number of years.

---

1. *Life of Theophilus and Maria*, pp166–167. See also the *Life of Priscus*, p183.

2. 'Emesea where he pretended to be a fool' (Leontius of Neapolis, *Life of Symeon the Fool*, p135); 'he was playing the fool' (p151); 'Abba Symeon played the fool' (p158); 'while seeming not to understand, while playing the fool' (p161); 'Abba Symeon, playing the idiot' (p163); 'immediately Symeon played the fool' (p165); 'he was [only] playing the fool' (p168). See also p153, p167.

3. See *Life of Symeon the Fool*, p159.

4. Ibid., p163.

5. *Vie de Syméon le Nouveau Théologien*, 55, p72.

6. Ibid., 55, p74.

7. *Vie de Cyrille le Philéote*, XV, p86.

8. *Life of St Sabbas the Younger*, pp218–221.

SCRIPTURAL FOUNDATIONS

We can see in those prophets who engaged in odd behavior the ancestors of the fools for Christ.[1] Thus for example we have Isaiah, who walked around naked and shoeless for three years to forewarn of the coming captivity of the Egyptian soldiers (*Isaiah* 20:2-3); Ezekiel, who slept before a brick symbolizing captive Jerusalem and ate bread cooked on human dung (*Ezech.* 4), and Osee, who symbolized by his marriage with a prostitute the infidelity of Israel towards God (*Osee* 3). These acts, by their non-conformist (and even scandalous), symbolic, and prophetic character, have a certain resemblance to some of the behavior of fools for Christ. They are however different: first, because they were momentary acts and not part of a over-all pattern of folly, not considered foolish by the individuals involved; second, by their purpose which is only to startle people's minds and awaken them to certain truths; third, by the fact that they were expressly ordered by God and responded to his intention within the framework of a prophetic function devolving upon their agent,[2] rather than the latter's ascetic will.

It is rather in the New Testament that it seems appropriate to seek the principal scriptural basis for foolishness in Christ.

In his letter to the Romans and his first letter to the Corinthians, St Paul emphasizes the diametrical opposition between the world's wisdom and God's to such an extent that

(1) what is wisdom in the eyes of the world is folly in the eyes of God: 'Professing themselves to be wise, they became fools.' (Rom. 1:22); 'Has not God made foolish the wisdom of this world?' (1 Cor. 1:20); 'For the wisdom of this world is foolishness with God' (1 Cor. 3:19).

(2) what is wisdom in the eyes of God is folly in the eyes of the world: 'The sensual man perceives not the things that are of the

---

1. I. Goraïnoff, *Les Fols en Christ*, pp15–16. J. Saward, *Dieu à la folie. Histoire des saints fous pour le Christ*, p15.
2. See *La Bible de Jérusalem*, Paris, 1961, 'Les Prophètes, Introduction', pp971–972.

Spirit of God' (1 Cor. 2:14); 'The word of the cross, to them indeed that perish, is foolishness' (1 Cor. 1:18); 'It pleased God by the foolishness of our preaching to save them that believe' (1 Cor. 1:21); 'We preach Christ crucified . . . unto the Gentiles foolishness' (1 Cor. 1:23); 'For the foolishness of God is wiser than men' (1 Cor. 1:25).

(3) what is folly in world's eyes is wisdom in God's: 'But the foolish things of the world God has chosen, that he may confound the wise' (1 Cor. 1:27).

Because wisdom according to God is foolishness to the world, Christ himself was treated as a madman (John 10:20) as well as St Paul (Acts 16:24). Thus either one can serve as models of the fools for Christ, those fervent Christians wishing to follow in the footsteps of their Master, to suffer all that as he had suffered, to be in everything, and therefore in this too, imitators of Christ and the saints, according to the recommendation of the Apostle: 'Be imitators of me, as I am of Christ' (1 Cor. 11:1; cf. 1 Cor. 4:16, Eph. 5:1, Phil. 3:17, 1 Thess. 1:6, 2 Thess. 3:7, 9).

Even more compelling is this statement by St Paul: 'But God has chosen the foolish things of the world' (1 Cor. 1:27), which seems to make foolishness-in-the-eyes-of-men a privileged way corresponding to an election by grace if not a divine calling.

It should be noted that St Paul lays claim to this foolishness: 'We are fools for Christ's sake' (1 Cor. 4:10), and recommends it in these terms: 'If anyone among you seem to be wise . . . let him become a fool, that he may be wise' (1 Cor. 3:18). Are not fools for Christ, or more precisely 'fools because of Christ', according to the very words of St Paul (*moroi dia Khriston*), Christians who have taken this latter recommendation as a commandment which they follow in every detail so to be able to say with the Apostle, 'We are fools for Christ's sake'?

It seems to us however that neither is the principal basis for foolishness in Christ to be found in these scriptural passages. The foolishness in these texts corresponds rather to the reversal of values effected by Christ, as is clear from the certain passages in the Gospels (especially Matt. 18:4, 20:16; Mark 9:35, 10:44; Luke 14:11). The

foolishness in this situation is taken in the spiritual and not psychopathological sense,[1] unless by analogy. It is in the same spiritual
sense that St John Cassian counsels: 'Make yourself foolish in this
world so that you may be wise';[2] that St Symeon the New Theologian notes: 'Those who are taught by God are considered morons by
the disciples of the wise of this age';[3] and that St Anthony tells us:

> A time is coming when men will go mad, and when they see
> someone who is not mad, they will attack him saying: 'You are
> mad, you are not like us.'[4]

Now fools for Christ are not considered as fools for the same reason that St Paul is so characterized either by himself or others. St
Paul, from the point of view of psychiatry, behaved in a sane manner, while the fools for Christ exhibit, as previously emphasized, a
pathological behavior which puts them in the same category as the
mentally ill or the possessed/insane. We will show in what follows
that, in every case, this foolishness is simulated with the chief intent
of incurring the humiliations that the insane have to endure in
almost all societies at the hands of their fellow citizens.

The scriptural basis for foolishness in Christ appears to reside
then in the general context of the formula 'we are fools for the sake
of Christ', namely throughout this passage from the first letter to the
Corinthians (4:9–13):

> For I think that God hath sent forth us apostles, the last as it
> were, men appointed to death; we are made a spectacle to the
> world, and to angels and to men. We are fools for Christ's sake
> but you are wise in Christ; we are weak, but you are strong; you
> are honorable, but we without honor. Even unto this hour we
> both hunger and thirst, and are naked and are buffeted, and have
> no fixed abode; and we labor, working with our own hands. We
> are reviled, and we bless. We are persecuted, and we suffer it. We

---

1. See the interpretation of St John Chrysostom, *Homilies on 1 Cor.*, 4:3.
2. *The Institutes*, IV, 41, 3.
3. *Practical and Theological Chapters*, III, 85.
4. *Apophthegmata*, alphabetical series, Anthony, 25.

are blasphemed, and we entreat. We are made as the refuse of this world, the offscouring of all even until now.

This parallel passage from the second letter to the Corinthians (6:8–10) can also be invoked as a basis:

By honor and dishonor; by evil report and good report; as deceivers, and yet true; as unknown, and yet known; as dying and, behold, we live; as chastised and not killed. As sorrowful, yet always rejoicing; as needy, yet enriching many; as having nothing, and possessing all things.

And the ninth Beatitude as well: 'Blessed are you when they shall revile you, and persecute you, and speak all that is evil against you, untruly, for my sake.' (Matt. 5:11)

We will see that this is the condition testified to by these words, with all the characteristics that they bring to mind, a condition sought for and assumed by the fools for Christ.[1]

Also notice that St Paul, in the previously cited passages, uses the word *moros* to designate a fool, but the word *salos* is most often used to designate a fool for Christ,[2] a term which in common speech means an 'ordinary' fool.

First Motive: Humility

The first and most fundamental reason that leads the *salos* to simulate madness is to draw contempt, humiliations and ill-treatment upon himself. This is quite explicit in the hagiographic accounts. Palladius notes this with regard to Isidora: she 'feigned madness and possession by a demon. And they detested her so much . . . , she preferring this'; not only did she take upon herself the most menial

---

1. Notice that the *Life of Symeon the Fool* makes appeal to these two just cited scriptural passages.

2. J. Grosdidier de Matons is quite rightly astonished, without understanding the motives for this difference: 'We should have expected the "fools for Christ" to be designated by a term more in line with the text of St Paul which served as the basis for this form of sanctity' (op. cit., p281).

work, becoming according to her biographer 'the monastery sponge,' but even accepted without complaint to be 'cuffed, insulted, cursed, and execrated.'[1] Theophilus and Maria constantly lived 'as mime-actors,' seeking to get hit on the head and have their ears boxed by the crowds that surrounded them.[2] Priscus, who consented to speak about himself to Abba John of Amida's envoy, said to him

> for the sake of the hope of my eternal life I am enduring labors and buffetings . . . ; I have much peacefulness, especially [from] the fact that I am reckoned a madman by them, and there is no one who speaks with me or who worries me.[3]

Antiochus, who had learned from a dream that he was spiritually a debtor, tells us:

> When I woke up I thought about my dream said . . . : 'Poor Antiochus! Still more hard work and dishonor for you!' Thereafter I pretended to be a fool. . . . When those pitiless fathers saw [this] they loaded all the heavy work of the monastery onto me.[4]

St Symeon multiplied extravagant and scandalous acts that, with few exceptions, were far from witnessing to the Kingdom whose values were opposed to this world, far from a breach of etiquette that manifests the 'unlimited freedom' of the saint,[5] but were so many provocations and, one could say, appeals for ill treatment. The manner in which he began his career as a *salos* is quite revealing in this regard. When he

> found a dead dog on a dunghill outside the city, he loosened the rope belt he was wearing, and tied it to the dog's foot. He dragged the dog as he ran and entered the gate, where there was a

---

1. Palladius, *Lausiac History*, XXXIV, 1 and 2.
2. *Life of Theophilus and Maria*, p 167.
3. *Life of Priscus*, p 183.
4. St John Climacus, *The Ladder*, IV, 121.
5. The study of C. Yannaras, *The Freedom of Morality*, trans. E. Briere (Crestwood: St Vladimir's Seminary Press, 1984), chapter 4, 'A Historical Example: The challenge of the "Fools in Christ"', pp 65–75 is centered on this brilliant interpretation, but is hardly in accord with the texts.

children's school nearby. When the children saw him, they began to cry, 'Hey, a crazy abba!' And they set about to run after him and box him on the ears. On the next day which was Sunday, he took nuts, and entering the Church at the beginning of the liturgy, he threw the nuts and put out the candles. When they hurried to run after him, he went up to the pulpit, and from there he pelted the women with nuts. With great trouble they chased after him, and when he was going out, he overturned the tables of the pastry chefs, who (nearly) beat him to death. Seeing himself crushed by the blows, he said to himself: 'Poor Symeon, if things like this keep happening, you won't live for a week in these people's hands.'[1]

In response to extravagant actions committed most often for this purpose, St Andrew was frequently maltreated: he was beaten, hit on the head with cudgels, his hair was pulled, he was spat upon, he was dragged through the streets by a cord tied to his neck and feet, he was slapped and had his face smeared with ink and charcoal, and people trod all over his body.[2] Hierotheus, from the monastery of St Symeon the New Theologian, assumed a form of insanity characterized by great clumsiness for, as Nicetas explains:

In his desire for mortification, he was often, by design, prone to overturning and even breaking the vessels he carried, so to hear insults or even, if necessary, be slapped squarely on the cheek. Overjoyed at such abuse, he was like someone at the peak of happiness. He even felt the need to be whipped.[3]

An episode in the life of St Cyril the Phileote shows him feigning mutism with the evident purpose of getting himself hit and put in prison to be mistreated.[4] The madness of St Sabbas the Younger, that also took the form of mutism, had the same purpose: to be mistreated. And in fact he was beaten to the point of death, stoned, covered with dust and rubbish, and people shouted:

1. *Life of Symeon the Fool*, p151.
2. Cf. *Life of Andrew Salos*, 16, PG 111, 648C-649A.
3. *Vie de Syméon le Nouveau Théologien*, 55.
4. *Vie de S. Cyrille le Philéote*, XV, 1–2.

Get away you idiot, you vagabond, you fool, you are crazy, a bird of ill omen, the scourge of the whole city; let him be beaten, stoned, and quickly driven from our borders.

St Sabbas sometimes performed inappropriate acts for the same purpose: thus once, with a cane that he held in his hand, he snatched and threw away a man's hat who, infuriated, beat him nearly to death.[1]

To obtain the same results, it is noteworthy that other ascetics (and sometimes those already mentioned) feigned other conditions which, in the surroundings where they found themselves, earned them contempt and similar ill-treatment. Isidora simulated possession as well as insanity.[2] Likewise Symeon allowed himself to be considered possessed by the devil.[3] A nun from the monastery of the Abba Jeremiah feigned drunkenness,[4] as did St Andrew.[5] Maria, the companion of Theophilus, pretended to be a prostitute and insane at the same time.[6]

And even more than madness, many of the *saloi* for the same reasons pretended to be sinners and allowed themselves to be accused of such without saying a word, thus accepting an unjustified bad reputation. Maria, for example, who lived disguised as a courtesan, allowed herself to be reproached as a fornicator even though she kept herself perfectly pure.[7] Symeon allowed himself to be unjustly accused of impregnating a young slave.[8]

By thus desiring contempt, humiliation and ill-treatment, the *salos* above all sought to achieve a high degree of humility. This goal, which to us is essential, seems to have eluded many of those who have

---

1. See *Life of St Sabbas the Younger*, pp, 224–225, 227, 233–234.
2. From indications of Palladius, it is not possible to decide if it is a question of insanity because of possession or of two distinct conditions manifesting themselves alternatively or together (*Lausiac History*, XXXIV, 1).
3. *Life of Symeon*, p153, p159.
4. *Vie et récits de l'abbé Daniel le Scétiote*, ed. du texte grec par L. Clugnet, *Revue de l'Orient chrétien*, 5, 1900, chap. VII, pp22–25.
5. *Life of Andrew Salos*, 70, PG 111, 712A.
6. *Life of Theophilus and Maria*, p166.
7. Ibid., p168.
8. *Life of Symeon the Fool*, p156.

studied foolishness for Christ. However, this is the interpretation which comes immediately to mind for Evagrius the Scholastic when he refers to the 'grazing' monks who return to the world in order to simulate folly. By this, according to him, these monks surmount the loftiest degree of the ascetic life, completely freed from *kenodoxia* or vainglory.[1] Archimandrite Sophrony, someone who well understood the eastern Christian ascetical life, says the same thing:

> The goal of the 'fool' is to be everyone's laughing-stock. Many are they who cannot understand this path and consider it a perversion. Yet, in its essence, it is the most sure means of getting rid of vainglory and thus winning a true victory over the world.[2]

This is reminiscent of these words of St Isaac the Syrian:

> A man who is truly humble is not troubled when he is wronged, and he says nothing to justify himself against the injustice, but he accepts slander as truth; he does not attempt to persuade men that he is calumniated, but he begs forgiveness. Some have voluntarily drawn upon themselves the repute of being licentious, while they are not such; others have endured the charge of adultery, being far from it, and proclaimed by their tears that they bear the fruit of the sin they had not committed, and have wept, asking their offenders' forgiveness for the iniquity they had not done, their souls all the while being crowned with all purity and chastity; others, lest they be glorified because of the virtuous state which they have hidden within them, have pretended to be lunatics, while in truth they were permeated with divine salt and securely fixed in serenity.[3]

(a) The *salos* seeks humility and accepts being scorned, rejected and considered as of no worth. This agrees with a traditional Patristic teaching.[4] According to St Macarius, it is the normal condition

---

1. *Ecclesiastical History*, I, 21.
2. 'Des fondements de l'ascèse orthodoxe', *Messager de l'exarchat du Patriarche russe en Europe occidentale*, 17, 1954, p35.
3. *Ascetical Homilies*, 6.
4. Cf. St Barsanuphius, *Letters*, 150. St John of Gaza, *Letters*, 307. St Isaac, *Ascetical Homilies*, 5; 57.

of Christians who

> are like men 'who carry in their hands their own blood' (Job
> 13:14), not . . . thinking themselves to be anything special. But
> they are neglected, condemned, and rejected among all men.[1]

Several Fathers teach that the person who afflicts, wrongs, or insults
us should be considered as a physician who heals us of vainglory
and pride.[2] One old man counsels: if the devil

> comes to mislead you into vainglory, do something or assume
> such an attitude that men will despise you. For, know well, Satan
> is never so desolate as when a person desires scorn and humilia-
> tions.[3]

St John Climacus tells us that 'the first step in overcoming vainglory
is to . . . accept dishonor gladly.'[4] And he says again with greater
clarity: 'God rejoices when he sees us running to meet dishonor, so
as to crush, strike, and destroy our vain self-esteem.'[5] St John of
Gaza notes 'Anyone who wants to obtain humility says "I want it" in
vain; if he cannot bear dishonor, he cannot obtain it.'[6] And St Barsanuphius remarks: 'This is perfect humility: put up with the out-
rages and injuries and all that our master Jesus suffered.'[7]

The humility which the *saloi* achieves is one of great solidity
because constantly tested against the standard of their relationship
with others—far more difficult to achieve and conserve than a
humility acquired inwardly and alone. As St Cyril the Phileote
notes, 'The tempest shows the pilot's worthiness, the stadium the
athlete's, the battle the general's, misfortune the magnanimous
man's, and temptation the Christian's.'[8] A sign that one is delivered
from vainglory is that one is no longer troubled when humiliated in

1. *Homilies* (Coll. II), XV, 26.
2. See *Apophthegmata*, XVI, 17, 18, and 19.
3. Ibid., N 592/54.
4. *The Ladder*, XXII, 39.
5. Ibid., XXV, 45.
6. *Letters*, 307.
7. *Letters*, 150.
8. *Vie de saint Cyrille le Philéote*, CV, 2.

public,[1] and no longer feels any bitterness against whoever has offended, disregarded, or insulted us.[2] Such is indeed what the biographers of the *saloi* tell us.

But this is also an extreme humility. The *saloi*, by their situation and their acts, put themselves squarely in a position to be considered the least of the least, and thus realize the classic monastic principle: 'Look upon yourselves as the least of all men.' Contempt of self, with a view to its total divestment, goes even to the point of self-degradation, as witnessed in some fairly symbolic situations.[3]

It is from this casting off of the old man that arises, according to the way of the *salos*, the life of the new man and his glorification. Here let us just recall this teaching of St Isaac the Syrian:

> Be contemptible in your own eyes, and you will see the glory of God in yourself. For where humility burgeons, there God's glory wells forth. If you strive to be slighted openly by all men, God will cause you to be glorified.[4]

Thus St Cyril the Phileote, who was imprisoned and mistreated after simulating madness and mutism said to himself:

> Do not object to the fullers: if they beat you by trampling you underfoot, if they stretch you out to comb you, at least by this your clothes will become sparkling; endure afflictions, for by these are woven crowns for those who struggle; If we willingly endure afflictions, curses will be transformed into blessings; just

---

1. See St John Climacus, *The Ladder*, XXI, 39.
2. See St Maximus the Confessor, *Centuries on Charity*, IV, 43.
3. Thus St. Andrew Salos: 'relieved himself in front of passers-by'; beaten by one of them, he fell prostrate before him and licked his feet 'like a dog' (*Life of Andrew Salos*, 68, PG 111, 708D–709B); to sleep, he sought out corners full of excrement where stray dogs sheltered (ibid.; 18, 649C; 65, 795B; 68, 79A). A nun from the convent of the Abba Jeremias who pretended to be drunk, passed the day lying on the ground for long periods of time, and at night she stood at the entrance to the latrines (*Vie et récits de l'abbé Daniel le Scétiote*, VII). St Sabbas the Younger would plunge into a foul sewer, coming out dirty and disgusting. (*Life of St Sabbas the Younger*, p 223).
4. *Ascetic Homilies*, 5.

as the hardship of the contest prepares crowns for the athletes, so too the ordeal of temptation leads Christians to perfection.[1]

With regard to Hierotheus, Nicetas Stethatos speaks of 'the perfection that he had attained through his care in profiting from contradictions and trials,'[2] which he himself had instigated, and notes that, by acting as he did, he thought that 'the blows dealt his exterior body would free the interior man from punishment in the age to come.'[3]

(b) The inappropriate or scandalous actions of the *salos* are a second aspect of the humility toward which he tends. They allow him to disguise his asceticism, hide his virtues, conceal his miracles, and thus avoid the glory that comes from men.

> The fathers of old did such things . . . that they might be dishonored, to hide the glory of their way of life, and to drive away from themselves the causes of pride.[4]

Thus, through humility, St Ammonas took refuge in feigned madness to avoid imparting judgments and advice to those that visited him.[5] The monk of the Abba Silvanus, a very strict ascetic in both body and soul, feigned madness in such a way as to turn everyone away from him[6] and live unknown to all.[7] The biographer of Theophilus and Maria tells us that he dressed in the costume of a mime and she in that of a courtesan, 'in order to deceive the spectators, lest anyone should perceive and know what they were.' Moreover, the elder Procopius who had induced them to lead this kind of life, recommended that they hide the great spiritual profit to be found in it.[8] It is said of St Symeon that 'his every prayer was that his works might be hidden until his departure from life, so that he might escape

1. *Vie de saint Cyrille le Philéote*, xv, 2.
2. *Vie de saint Syméon le Nouveau Théologien*, 56.
3. Ibid., 55.
4. *Ascetical Homilies*, 21.
5. *Apophthegmata*, alphabetical series, Ammonas, 9.
6. His biographer tells us that, when a brother met him, he set to laughing until the brother went away (John Rufus, *Plerophories*, p178).
7. Ibid., pp178–179.
8. *Life of Theophilus and Maria*, pp166 and 176.

human glory, through which human arrogance and conceit arises,'[1] and it was also his

> practice, whenever he did something miraculous, to leave that neighborhood immediately, until the deed he had done was for-gotten, [and] hurried on immediately elsewhere to do something inappropriate, so that he might thereby hide his perfection.

Thus, to destroy the good impression that he had made on a tavern keeper and prevent him telling about what he had done, while the tavern-keeper was busy, Symeon went up to the room where his wife was sleeping and started to undress. She began to cry rape and the furious husband threw him out. Moreover Symeon's biographer tells us that

> without tasting bread all week, the righteous one often ate meat. No one knew about his fasting, since he ate meat in front of everybody in order to deceive them.[2]

Many of his miracles were performed in an indirect manner through extravagant behavior, in such a way that he was not per-ceived to be their cause. Before relating one of these miracles, his biographer makes it clear that

> the all-wise Symeon's whole goal was this: first, to save souls . . . second, that his virtue not be known, and he receive neither approval nor honor from men.[3]

Symeon's end was worthy of one who was a fool for Christ through-out his life. Having been made aware of the time of his departure for the next world, and

> not wanting to obtain human honor after his death, what did he do? He went inside, lay down to sleep underneath the bundle of twigs in his sacred hut.

His acquaintances finding him

1. *Life of Symeon the Fool*, p150.
2. Ibid., p153.
3. Ibid, p161.

lying dead under his bundle of twigs ... said, 'Now all will believe that he was beside himself. Behold his death is another idiocy.'[1]

The *Life* of St Sabbas the Younger shows him setting off anew to feign madness because offended by the honors rendered him.[2] And his biographer tells us that he adopted this manner of living 'to hide as much as possible the treasures of spiritual wisdom abiding in him.'[3]

The *saloi* also take great care to hide the place where they retire for the night so to devote themselves, in peace and solitude, to prayer.[4]

They begged those holy people who saw through their disguise not to reveal their secret.[5] Theophilus and Maria told John of Ephesus that if he showed them any respect in public other than as in their adopted roles, he would not see them again.[6] Likewise Priscus who, after revealing to a messenger of the abbot what he was, said to him:

> See that you do not make yourself the cause of my moving from this city. ... And beg the abbot that, though these things are known to him, he will leave me as I am and not show any difference towards me.[7]

And when, despite their efforts at dissimulation, it was discovered that they were counterfeiting madness, when the quality of their interior life was perceived, or when their miracles earned them recognition and veneration, they fled and hastened to some unknown place. Palladius reports that St Isidora, after having been exposed by St Piteroum,

---

1. Ibid., p169.
2. *Life of St Sabbas the Younger*, p241.
3. Ibid., p222.
4. Cf. *Life of Symeon the Fool*, p163. *Life of Theophilus and Maria*, p171. *Life of Andrew Salos*, PG 111, 712A–C.
5. See, *Life of Theophilus and Maria*, p170.
6. Ibid., p177.
7. *Life of Priscus*, p183.

unable to bear her glory and the honor bestowed by the sisters, and burdened by their apologies, she left the monastery. And where she went . . . or how she died, no one knows.[1]

The same was true of the anonymous nun from the convent of Abba Jeremias. Her holiness having been discovered by Daniel and revealed to the superiors and other sisters, she fled the convent.[2] St Sabbas the Younger left the place where he had taken up residence every time that his virtues were recognized and he began to be venerated.[3]

In some cases the reason for simulating madness was penitential, but it is precisely a matter of penitence accomplished by way of humiliation.

One of St Mark the Fool's chief motivations for choosing this state was to compensate for a period of his life in which the passion of lust prevailed, as he himself relates:

I was dominated by the demon of lust for some fifteen years, but I came to myself and said: 'Mark, you have been a slave to the Enemy for fifteen years; now be a servant of Christ for just as long'; and I took the habit at Pempton and remained there eight years. But after these eight years I said to myself: 'Now go to the city and act as a fool for eight more years.'[4]

Here foolishness for Christ seems to complete and even surpass the monastic lifestyle, and this, one supposes, as a result of the humiliations involved. This is to be met with again and seems beyond question in the life of Antiochus. This monk, having known by a dream that he owed a spiritual debt, in order to wipe out the debt lived 'three years in [a] monastery in total obedience, despised by everyone, [and] insulted as a foreigner.' Warned by a second dream that only a tenth of his debt had been paid, he tells us

1. *Lausiac History*, xxxxiv, 7.
2. *Vie et récits de l'abbé Daniel le Scétiote*, vii.
3. *Life of St Sabbas the Younger*, pp 243, 258, 263, 292, 298.
4. *Vie de Marc le Fou*, p 61.

I thought about my dream and said: 'Only ten! How will I ever pay the rest?' After that I said: 'Poor Antiochus! Still more hard work and dishonor for you!' Thereafter I pretended to be a fool.[1]

SECOND MOTIVE: DETACHMENT FROM THIS WORLD

The condition of being a fool for Christ seems to be a means of holding 'this world' in derision. Informing his companion John about his vocation, Symeon told him: 'I will go in the power of Christ; I will mock the world.'[2] There is, in the mockery of the *salos* and in his scandalous acts, an ironic dispute with this fallen world and its limitations, and also with the various forms of attachment shown with respect to it.

But even more than words and acts, it is by the very nature of the condition that he has chosen to assume that the fool for Christ realizes in himself a high degree of detachment from the world by means of three traits favored by this state, namely, solitude (exterior and interior), the status of stranger, and poverty.

Solitude

Abba Or seems to make simulated madness the ascetic equivalent in the world of the eremetic life when he advises: 'Either flee the world completely, or make fun of the world and people by playing the fool most of the time.'[3]

This may seem paradoxical for, although it is true that when night comes the *saloi* desire seclusion, taking refuge in some place known to them alone, during the day they seek on the contrary to be in contact with the inhabitants of the city where they have chosen to

---

1. St John Climacus, *The Ladder*, IV, 121.
2. *Life of Symeon the Fool*, p148.
3. *Apophthegmata*, alphabetical series, Or, 14, PG 65, 440C. Cf. *Apophthegmata*, anonymous series, 188: 'An old man said: "Either you should flee from men in reality, or you are ridiculing the world and men by making yourself in all things fool."'

reside. Besides one cannot be a fool for Christ in isolation, for this condition only makes sense within a social context and in relationship to others.

But it is precisely this madness that assures the *salos* true isolation even in the midst of a crowd: it brings rejection by all—no one knowing what he really is—and it prevents people from having an ordinary and 'normal' relationship with him.[1]

The Status of Stranger

The *Saloi* frequently go and live far from their place of birth, for they wish to remain strangers,[2] just as they are interiorly estranged from the world. Thus they practice to a high degree the virtue of *xeniteia* so highly extolled by the Fathers.[3] The biographer of St Sabbas the Younger tells us that

> he never remained in a fixed place for any length of time, but preferred to engage in divine contemplation in the desert, the mountains, caves, and in the dens of wild beasts. He would then reappear in one or another city, countryside, or village, mixing with the crowds, festivals, and markets so that he seemed to daily join in with the crowds, but was in reality totally separated from men, not only in his heart by his great spiritual withdrawal, but by the fact that, going along everywhere in this complete silence and with this attitude, he was virtually unknown, as if he were being seen for the first time.[4]

1. See the *Life of St Sabbas the Younger*, p 217 (cited in the following paragraph).

2. This was the case with Symeon. See also the *Life of Theophilus and Maria*, p 176; *Life of Priscus*, p 183; *The Story of Antiochus*, in St John Climacus, *The Ladder*, IV, 121.

3. Cf. *Apophthegmata*, alphabetical series, Andrew. St John Climacus, *The Ladder*, III, 1–34. With regard to this propensity, see A. Guillaumont, 'Le dépaysement comme forme d'ascèse dans le monachisme ancien', in: École pratique des hautes études, Vᵉ section, Sciences religieuses, *Annuaire*, 1968-1969, t. LXXVI, Paris, 1968, pp 31–58, reprinted in *Aux origins du monachisme chrétien*, Bellefontaine, 1979, pp 89–116.

4. *Life of St Sabbas the Younger*, p 217.

Poverty

With regard to their circumstances, all the *saloi* lived in extreme poverty and deprivation. St Isidora fastened rags on her head in place of a cowl and lived on crumbs from the table and what she scoured from the kitchen pots.[1] St Mark the Fool wore only a simple loin cloth and spent the night on public benches.[2] The anonymous nun from the monastery of Abba Jeremias dressed in rags.[3] St Symeon retired at night to a little hut in which there was 'nothing but a bundle of twigs.'[4] St Andrew Salos dressed in tattered rags and led the life of a vagabond.[5] St Sabbas the Younger lived almost naked and had no place to lie down and sleep.[6] André-Jean Festugière thinks there were two reasons why Sabbas chose to live in a state of nakedness: to be subject to the changes of weather, and to become, by his miserable appearance, an object of contempt.[7]

There are numerous examples of the *saloi* refusing alms[8] or quickly making a gift of them to others. Mark the Fool, who received a meager salary for his work, kept only a tenth for his own nourishment and gave the rest to other fools.[9] Priscus refused the clothes offered him for winter.[10]

THIRD MOTIVE: CHARITY

Another important reason that induced certain ascetics to become fools for Christ is that this condition is most propitious for the exercise of charity, particularly with regard to the most deprived.

1. Palladius, *Lausiac History*, XXXIV, 1; 3; 5.
2. *Vie de Marc le Fou*, p 60.
3. *Vie et récits de l'abbé Daniel le Scétiote*, VII.
4. *Life of Symeon the Fool*, p 168.
5. See *Life of Andrew Salos*, 18, PG 111, 649C; 65, 705B; 68, 709A.
6. *Life of St Sabbas the Younger*, pp 216, 219–221.
7. A.–J Festugière, 'Etude sur la vie de of S. Sabbas le Jeune qui simulait la folie', p 240.
8. See *Life of Priscus*, p 180. *Life of St Sabbas the Younger*, p 217.
9. *Vie et récits de l'abbé Daniel le Scétiote*, III, p 60.
10. *Life of Priscus*, p 181.

This motive is not first for the two preceding motives are common to all *saloi*, while this latter motive is only manifested with those who have chosen to live in the cities. It seemed essential in the choice of St Symeon. After having passed thirty-one years as a hermit in the desert with his companion John, Symeon said to him:

'What more benefit do we derive, brother, from passing time here in this desert? But if you hear me, get up, let us depart; let us save others. For as we are, we do not benefit anyone except ourselves, and have not brought anyone else to salvation.' And he began to quote to him from the Holy Scriptures such things as 'Let no one seek his own good, but rather the good of his neighbor' (1 Cor. 10:24.), and again 'All things to all men, that I might save all' (1 Cor. 9:22).[1]

And his biographer notes

The all-wise Symeon's whole goal was this: first, to save souls. . . .[2] For it was not thought just that the one thus honored by God and placed high should disdain the salvation of his fellow men, but remembering the one who said, 'Love your neighbor as yourself' (Luke, 10:27), who did not disdain to put on the form of a slave, although unchanged, for the salvation of a slave (cf. Phil. 2:6 ff), Symeon imitated his master and truly used his own soul and body to save others.[3]

It is typical of the *saloi* who had this goal to feign, then, a kind of insanity that favored its accomplishment, that is, in place of retreating within themselves they on the contrary favored contact with others. Thus St Symeon, St Andrew, and, as far as we can judge, St Mark were hyperactive, exuberant, and talkative fools.

These *saloi* showed themselves particularly compassionate over the ills and miseries of the poorest, the humiliated, and those held in contempt by society, insofar as they themselves continually experienced the same lot. Their condition permitted them more easily

1. *Life of Symeon the Fool*, p148.
2. Ibid., p161.
3. Ibid., Prologue, pp133–134.

than anyone else to approach and keep them company, to be accepted as one of them, to inspire their sympathy and gain their confidence. Thus St Mark the Fool had as his usual companions the village fools and used nine-tenths of his salary to feed them.[1] The biographer of Symeon shows him 'sitting with his brothers in poverty.'[2] He showed himself singularly attentive to the conditions of prostitutes; his impassibility allowed him to frequent these woman in complete chastity, and his 'folly' allowed him to take on the scandal that this caused.[3]

He often brought some disreputable women and prostitutes to lawful marriage through his jesting; others he made chaste after captivating them with money; then he spurred them on to pursue the monastic life by means of the purity he had acquired.[4]

He also

had extraordinary compassion for those possessed by demons, so that from time to time he went off to make himself like one of them, and passed his time with them, healing many of them through his own prayer.[5]

And he advised his friend, John the deacon:

I beg you, never disregard a single soul, especially when it happens to be a . . . beggar. For Your Charity knows that His place is among the beggars, especially among the blind, people made as pure as sun through their patience and distress. Such country peasants as I often saw in the city, coming in to receive communion, are purer than gold on account of their innocence and simplicity, and by the sweat of their brow, they eat their bread. . . . Show love for your neighbor through almsgiving. . . . For [Scripture] says, 'Blessed is he who meets with the poor, the Lord delivers him on the evil day' (Ps. 40:2).[6]

---

1. See *Vie de Marc le Fou*, p60.
2. *Life of Symeon the Fool*, p165.
3. See Ibid., pp159–161.
4. Ibid., p150.
5. Ibid., p165.
6. Ibid., pp168–169.

The solicitude of the fools for Christ is not however limited to those who were humble or on the margins of society, but is held out to anyone in difficulty. Leontius tells us that Symeon healed those who were possessed by demons or ill, converted to the faith those who did not believe or were heretics, or rescued others who were in danger,[1] and he gives us many other examples of his charity.

This charity was often manifested with regard to sinners. The care with which they redressed them was a common trait with both Symeon and Andrew.[2] For this they used seemingly insane words and acts, but which had in fact a hidden logic, were perfectly adapted to their purpose, and undoubtedly achieved this better than the admonitions of clergy or well-meaning laity.[3] Their words and actions often had a symbolic character which encouraged the person to whom they were addressed to reflect, and were in turn followed by wonderful effects because of the miraculous power of the saint.[4] Under cover of insanity, mockery was often used as a salutary irony which could be exercised on all without regard for convention or social hierarchy.[5] Folly also permitted the *salos* to transgress certain social norms, like property rights, by actions that were formally immoral but which were symbolically an invitation to share with as well as a means to come to the aid of the destitute. St Mark the fool 'would grab whatever he found in the market-place and give it to the other fools'[6] St Symeon, hired as a salesman for a commercial enterprise, freely distributed the contents of the store to the poor.[7]

---

1. Ibid., 150.

2. For this latter especially see the *Life of Andrew Salos*, 57-59, PG 111, 696D–700C; 106–113, 749B–760B; 153, 800D–801A; 205–207, 849B–852C.

3. This was a constant feature in the *Life of Symeon the Fool*, but more rare in the *Life of Andrew Salos* (see 16, PG 111, 648CD; 77, 717A–C; 115, 760D–761A). As J. Grosdidier de Matons remarks (op. cit., p 305) Andrew expressed this almost always 'in preaching and in a moral sense, not as *salos*'.

4. See *Life of Symeon the Fool*, p155; p164;, p165; p166. Cf. *Life of Andrew Salos*, PG 111, 717A–C and 720D–724A; 744C–748B.

5. See *Life of Symeon the Fool*, pp157–158. It should be noted that a *salos* is inwardly deeply respectful of those he mocks: Symeon jeered at monks particularly (p157) but recommended to his friend John 'never disregard a single soul, especially . . . a monk' (p168).

6. *Vie de Marc le Fou*, p 60.

7. *Life of Symeon the Fool*, p151.

This charity was always exercised in close relationship to the virtue of humility which, as we have shown, was the principal concern of the *salos*. In this connection Leontius notes that Symeon 'did not want to do anything in a clear manner; instead he always did things through clowning,'[1] and relates that

> he pretended to babble, for he said of all semblances, this one is most fitting and most useful to those who simulate folly for the sake of Christ. For this reason, often he reproved and restrained sins, and he sent divine wrath to someone to correct him, and he made predictions and did everything he wanted.... In all that he did, they believed that he was just like the many who babbled and prophesied because of demons.[2]

In this manner, Leontius tells us, Symeon 'nearly put an end to sinning in the whole city.'[3]

Let us finally note that the *saloi* often possessed charisms of discernment (*diakrisis*), clairvoyance (*diorasis*), and prophecy (*proorasis*) because of their great interior purity and humility. These, with very rare exceptions,[4] were exercised in relationship with their love of neighbor and their concern to come to their assistance.[5]

Spiritual Presuppositions of Foolishness for Christ

Foolishness for Christ involves a quite exceptional way of life. To adopt this path presumes that several conditions be fulfilled.

A Call from God or a Personal Vocation Approved by God

Theophilus and Maria were invited to follow this way of life by the old man Procopius who told them that this was the will of God, and

1. Ibid., p167.
2. Ibid., pp159. Cf. p165.
3. Ibid., p165.
4. See ibid., p155.
5. See ibid., pp152–153, 154, 155, 157, 159-160, 161.

they considered that they had assumed their disguise with God's help.[1] John of Amida saw in Priscus 'one of those "poor in spirit" to whom a blessing was given by our Lord.'[2] When Symeon informed his companion John about his vocation, the latter tried to discourage him, but without success. Leontius notes that then 'he knew that he had been convinced by God to do this,' and Symeon actually declares this: 'It is not by my own [will] that I wish to do this, but because God commands me.'[3] It was with the blessing of his spiritual father Nicephorus that St Andrew undertook the feigning of madness.

An Already Highly Accomplished Spiritual Life

In their *Lives* the *saloi* appear as great ascetics. First of all we observe that they ate and slept very little. Thus St Isidora's biographer relates: 'None of the four hundred sisters ever saw her chewing during the years of her life. She never sat at table, nor partook of a piece of bread, but wiping up the crumbs from the tables and washing the kitchen pots she was content with what she got in this way.'[4] On the subject of the 'Grazers' who came into the world to feign insanity, Evagrius wrote: They do not allow themselves 'to partake to satiety in any necessary. Indeed, their own rule enjoins them to hunger and thirst, and to clothe the body only so far as necessity requires.'[5] St Symeon Salos ate only one day a week and abstained from nourishment during almost the whole of Lent.[6]

Time taken from sleep is devoted to prayer. Leontius tells us that Symeon 'passed the night without sleeping, praying until morning, drenching the ground with his tears.'[7] Theophilus and Maria prayed for long periods of time and made many prostrations before taking

---

1. *Life of Theophilus and Maria*, pp172, 175–176.
2. *Life of Priscus*, p179.
3. *Life of Symeon the Fool*, p149.
4. Palladius, *Lausiac History*, XXXIV, 2.
5. Evagrius, *Ecclesiastical History*, I, 21.
6. *Life of Symeon the Fool*, pp153, 160.
7. Ibid., p168.

a little rest.[1] as did the 'Grazers' that Evagrius[2] speaks about. St Andrew practiced unceasing prayer throughout the day and, in addition, prayed at night before or in the churches.[3]

Moreover their *Lives* show them as possessed of perfect impassibility. Isidora, 'although she was cuffed and insulted and cursed and execrated', 'never did she insult any one nor grumble nor talk either little or much.'[4] The 'Grazers'

> study the art of apathy in eating, practising it even, if need be, with the petty retailers of victuals. They also constantly frequent the public baths, mostly mingling and bathing with women, since they have attained to such an ascendancy over their passions, as to possess dominion over nature, and neither by sight, touch, or even embracing of the female, to relapse into their natural condition.[5]

Symeon and Andrew showed themselves completely insensitive to sights quite capable of arousing concupiscence. Having once entered into the steam-baths reserved for women, Symeon described the nature of his interior state in these words:

> Just as a piece of wood goes with other pieces of wood, thus was I there. For I felt neither that I had a body nor that I had entered among bodies, but the whole of my mind was on God's work, and I did not part from Him.[6]

Leontius tells us moreover that he

> had advanced to such a degree of purity and impassivity that often he skipped and danced, holding hands with one dancing-girl on this side and another on that, and he associated with them and played with them in the middle of the whole circus, so that the disreputable women threw their hands into his lap, fondled

1. *Life of Theophilus and Maria*, p169.
2. *Ecclesiastical History*, I, 21.
3. *Life of Andrew Salos*, PG 111, 652BC and 712A–C.
4. Palladius, *Lausiac History*, XXXIV, 2.
5. Evagrius, *Ecclesiastical History*, I, 21.
6. *Life of Symeon the Fool*, p154.

him, poked him, and pinched him. But the monk like pure gold, was not defiled by them at all.[1]

We find a comparable passage in the *Life of Andrew*, where the saint, who had been dragged by force to a brothel, was seen to be perfectly impassable in the face of verbal and physical solicitations by prostitutes.[2] The biographer of St Symeon notes in a general manner that

> he rose to the most pure and impassible height, although to those more impassioned and more fleshly he seemed to be a defilement, a sort of poison, and an impediment to the virtuous life on account of his appearance. Because of these things he was most pure, just as a pearl which has traveled through slime unsullied.[3]

Having achieved the summit of *praxis* and having acquired *apatheia*, the *saloi* have access to the highest realms of contemplation. Many of them have even been seen shining with the divine light while at prayer.[4] Their sanctity was moreover recognized by those spiritual people blessed with the gift of discernment or to whom these things were revealed.[5]

It should be stressed that when the *saloi* started to feign madness, they were not beginners in the spiritual life, but often already had behind them a long period of ascetic endeavor and had attained a high degree of spiritual accomplishment. The 'Grazers' mentioned by Evagrius 'had achieved a state of impassibility because of their virtues before returning to the world.[6] Mark of Alexandria had lived eight years in a monastery.[7] Antiochus also had numerous years of monastic life behind him and, during the last three of these, had

---

1. Ibid., p159.
2. *Life of Andrew Salos*, 20–21, PG 111, 652C–653C.
3. *Life of Symeon the Fool*, Prologue, pp132–133.
4. *Life of Priscus*, pp181–182. *Life of Symeon the Fool*, p163. *Life of Andrew Salos*, 38–39, PG 111, 672D–676A.
5. Cf. Palladius, *Lausiac History*, XXXIV, 3 and 6 (Isidora), *Vie de Marc le Fou*, p61. John Rufus, *Plrophories*, pp178–179 (the monk of Abba Silvanus). *Life of Symeon the Fool*, pp135 and162.
6. Evagrius, *Ecclesiastical History*, I, 21.
7. *Vie de Marc le Fou*, p61.

submitted to a particularly harsh ascesis.[1] St Symeon spent thirty years as a hermit in the desert by the Dead Sea with his companion John, and his biographer tells us:

> This was not someone undisciplined, still lacking a trainer, who has gone toward the world, but . . . because he was fighting the noble battle well and in accordance with the law, because he saw that he had been armed with the power of the spirit, because he had acquired the power to trample snakes and scorpions under foot [Luke 10:19], because he quenched the burning of the flesh with the dew of the Holy Spirit, because he spat upon all the softness and sentiment of life as on a spider . . . and because he put impassivity upon himself as a garment, both inside and outside, on account of his humility . . . he went forth out of the desert and into the world, as into single combat against the Devil.[2]

The biographer of St Sabbas the Younger notes that

> it was not straight away and without preparation that [he] decided to engage in this manner of action, this pretence of insanity, but it was only after having controlled all his members and all his senses, to the point that nowhere in him did what was inferior rebel against what was superior, that he sprang with suitable confidence towards this manner of sporting with the artful Lord of malice;[3] he had first, by self-mastery and humility, excellently healed the illness of his soul . . . and it is only then that he dared to undertake this new course and new struggle.[4]

The possession of impassibility (*apatheia*), a state that crowns such an ascetic life and that consists in being purified of all passion, is an preliminary, indispensable condition for taking upon oneself the way of foolishness for Christ. If not the risk of embracing this way of life through pride and drawing pride rather than humility from it is very great. The second risk, as John stressed to his companion

1. Cf. St John Climacus, *The Ladder*, V, 121.
2. *Life of Symeon the Fool*, Prologue, p 133.
3. *Life of St Sabbas the Younger*, p 235.
4. Ibid., p 221.

Symeon, is to be troubled by the acts that will be committed, the words uttered, and the situations endured in this condition.[1] The third risk is to become genuinely insane and possessed, the devil profiting from the spiritual weakness of the *salos* to overawe him and suggest acts and words. Thus patriarch Philotheus Kokkinos, author of the *Life of St Sabbas the Younger* recalls certain individuals who

> were unknowingly led astray, who did not 'play' at madness, but actually became insane both in their words and actions, and who instead of 'making fun of the demons and the world', according to the expression of the Fathers, themselves ended up becoming an object of deception and laughter. For, since they had not as yet submitted the irrational part of their souls to reason, nor completely given the reins to the better part, and had thus prematurely left the starting-line, they easily fell from the precipice of their passions, saying and doing in an indecent manner what is natural for a true fool to say and do.[2]

One might think that these considerations contradict our thesis: if the *saloi* have attained to the state of impassibility and thus humility before embracing this life, it makes little sense to affirm that they were essentially seeking humility in this life. They in fact sought to achieve 'the utmost degree of humility'. The biographer of St Priscus presents this way as fostering the attainment of excellence.[3] Evagrius the Scholastic considered it the highest form of asceticism, a final step that few ascetics are able to clear.[4] St John Climacus notes that the characteristics appropriate to the perfect are: 'they are humble, they long for dishonor, they look out for involuntary sufferings'; he also notes: 'virtue of this sort comes only from a complete abandonment of the world and only the really great can endure the derision of their own folk.' And again he writes: 'If the outer limit, the rule,

---

1. *Life of Symeon the Fool*, p149.
2. *Life of St Sabbas the Younger*, pp 221–222. The criticism of false fools for Christ found on these pages is also found in the *Catecheses* (XXVIII, ll. 369–381) of St Symeon the New Theologian.
3. *Life of Priscus*, p179.
4. *Ecclesiastical History*, I, 21.

and the characteristic of extreme pride is for a man to make a show of having virtues he does not actually possess for the sake of glory, then surely the token of extreme humility will be to lower ourselves by claiming weaknesses we do not really have.'[1] St Isaac the Syrian says with regard to the fools for Christ: theirs is an 'uttermost perfection'.[2] Archimandrite Sophrony tells us that 'foolishness for Christ [is a] spiritual feat that especially manifests the third [and highest] degree of renunciation,' renunciation of vainglory.[3] I. Kovalesky speaks of a 'supererogatory' ascetic feat, a possibility not offered by ordinary monastic life.[4]

Conclusion

Lastly it would appear that foolishness for Christ constitutes a special ascetic path enabling the individual to realize three Christian virtues: humility, detachment from the world, and charity.[5] The *salos* uses simulated madness to seek out and experience the first by means of humiliations which this counterfeited state draws upon him in surroundings rather intolerant of fools, to realize the second by making himself a wretch and a pariah, to practice the third hidden from the eyes of the world, and by keeping as close as possible to most destitute. All the characteristics generally recognized in the

---

1. *The Ladder,* VII, 6; XXV, 43; XXV, 41.

2. *Ascetical Homilies,* 6.

3. 'Des fondements de l'ascèse orthodoxe,' *Messager de l'exarchat du Patriarche russe en Europe occidentale,* 17, 1954, p 35.

4. *Jurodstvo o Xriste i Xrista radi jurodivye,* Moscou, 1900, p 103, n 1.

5. This suffices to distinguish the Christian *salos* from analogous types to be encountered in other traditions, like the cynic of Greek philosophy (see T. Goritcheva, 'Cynisme, folie en Christ et sainteté,' *Contacts,* 134, 1986, pp 90–107), the Hindu *pasupata* (cf. A.Y. Syrkin, 'On the behavior of the "Fools for Christ's Sake"', *History of Religions,* 22, 1982, p 166), or the Islamic *majthub* (see A. Bausani, 'Note sul "pazzo sacro" nell'Islam,' *Studi e materiali di storia delle religioni,* 29, 1958, pp 93–107).

saloi can be connected, in our opinion, to one or another of these three virtues.[1]

However, this detachment achieved in extreme poverty and by becoming a stranger (*xeniteia*) can just as well be lived in the ordinary monastic state, especially the eremetic. As to charity for those on society's fringes, it can be exercised secretly outside of the status of fool,[2] but it also only characterizes the *saloi* living in cities. As a result the only characteristic common to all *saloi* and truly specific to their state seems to be a maximalist search for humility, constantly experienced through the disdain, humiliations, and sufferings unjustly endured 'for Christ'.

1. The studies of T. Spidlik ('"Fous pour Christ" en Orient', *Dictionnaire de spiritualité*, t. V, 1964, col. 753–757) and J. Saward (*Dieu à la folie. Histoire des saints fous pour le Christ*, 1983, pp 42–49) clearly identify the chief characteristics of foolishness for Christ, but are flawed in not seeing their connection.

2. In this respect the *Life of St John of Cyprus* tells of a typical case, that of the monk Vitalius who takes a job in the city and, when evening comes, spends his time drawing prostitutes away from their condition, using his salary to pay them not to fornicate and praying for their conversion, asking them to not disclose his mode of acting, and even letting himself be unjustly accused of having one or another from among them as a mistress (Leontius of Neapolis, *Vie de Jean de Chypre*, XXXVI, éd. commentée par A.-J. Festugière (Paris: Librarie Orientaliste Paul Geuthner, 1974), pp 69–75 of the Gelzer edition. [This chapter is not translated in Norman H. Baynes' 1948 English edition.]

BIBLIOGRAPHY

Patristic Sources

Apophtegmata:

Alphabetical series: PG 65, 71–440, completed by J.-C. guy, *Recherches sur la tradition grecque des Apophtegma Patrum*, 'Subsidia Hagiographica' no. 36, Bruxelles, 1962, pp 19–36. French trans. J.-C. Guy, *Les Apophtegmes des Pères du désert. Série alphabétique*, 'Spiritualité orientale' no. 1, Bellefontaine, 1966, pp 17–317. English trans. B. Ward, *The Sayings of the Desert Fathers*, rev. ed. (Kalamazoo, Michigan: Cistercian Publications, 1984).

Anonymous series. Greek text edited by F. Nau, *Revue de l'Orient chrétien*, 12–14 and 17–18, 1907–1913. Trans. B. Ward, *The Wisdom of the Desert Fathers* (Fairacres, Oxford: SLG Press, 1986).

Unpublished or little known Apophtegmata collected and presented by Dom L. Regnault. Translated from Greek (N, PE), Latin (R, Pa, M), Syriac (Bu), Armenian (Arm), Coptic (Eth Coll), and Ethiopian (Eth Coll, Eth Pat) by the monks of Solesmes, *Les Sentences des Pères du désert. Nouveau Recueil*, Solesmes, 1970.

Additions to the alphabetico-anonymous collection, additions to the systematic Greek collection (I–XXI, H, QRT), apophtegmata translated from Latin (PA, CSP), apophtegmata translated from Coptic (Am) by Dom L. Regnault, *Les Sentences des Pères du désert. Troisième recueil*, Solesmes, 1976.

Arsenius, *Letter*. Trans. by B. Outtier in *Lettres des Pères du désert*, 'Spiritualité orientale' no. 42, Bellefontaine, 1985, pp 107–113.

Athanasius of Alexandria, *Against the Heathen*. Vol. IV, Nicene and Post-Nicene Fathers, series II, P. Schaff (ed.) (New York: Christian Literature Publishing Co., 1892).

———. *Life of Anthony*. PG 26, 835–976. Vol. IV, Nicene and Post-Nicene Fathers, series II, P. Schaff (ed.), (New York: Christian Literature Publishing Co., 1892).

Barsanuphius, *Letters*. Edition of Nicodemus the Hagiorite, Venice, 1816, reprinted by S. N. Schoinas, Volos, 1960. French translation by Dom

L. Regnault, P. Lemaire et B. Outtier in Barsanuphe et Jean, *Correspondance*, Solesmes, 1972.

Basil of Caesarea, *Ascetic Constitutions*. PG 31, 1321–1428.

_____, *On the Origin of Man*. (Hom. x and xi of the Hexameron), critical text and French trans. A. Smets and M. Van Esbroeck, 'Sources chrétiennes', no. 160, Paris, 1970.

Callinicos, *Life of Hypatios*. Critical text and French translation by G. J. M. Bartelink, 'Sources chrétiennes', no. 177, Paris, 1971.

Clement of Alexandria, *The Instructor*. Ante-Nicene Fathers, vol. 2. A. Roberts and J. Donaldson (eds.), American Edition, 1885.

Cyril of Scythopolis, *Life of St Sabbas*. Text established by E. Schwartz, *Texte und Untersuchungen*, XLIX 2, Leipzig-Berlin, 1939. French trans. A.-J. Festugière, *Les Moines d'Orient*, III/2, Paris, 1961.

_____, *Life of Abraamios*. Text established by E. Schwartz, *Texte und Untersuchungen*, XLIX 2, Leipzig-Berlin, 1939. French trans. A-J. Festugière, *Les Moines d'Orient*, III/3, Paris, 1963.

Dionysius the Areopagite, *The Ecclesiastical Hierarchy*, PG 3, 396–569, trans. C. Luibheid and P. Rorem, *Pseudo-Dionysius. The Complete Works* (New York: Paulist Press, 1987), pp 195–259.

Diadochos of Photiki, *On Spiritual Knowledge and Discrimination: 100 Texts*. Trans. G. E. H. Palmer, P. Sherrard, K. Ware, in *The Philokalia*, vol. 1 (London/Boston: Faber and Faber, 1979), pp 253–296.

Dorotheos of Gaza, *Discourses*, trans. E. P. Wheeler (Kalamazoo, Michigan: Cistercian Publications, 1977), pp 77–211.

_____, *Maxims*. Ibid., pp 251–253.

Epiphanius of Cyprus, *Panarion*. PG 41, 173–1200 and PG 42, 9–773.

Evagrius Ponticus, *Antirrheticos*. Syriac text with Greek retroversion edited by W. Frankenberg, *Evagrius Ponticus*, Berlin, 1912, pp 472–545.

_____, *Exhortation to a Virgin*. Edition H. Gressmann, *Texte und Untersuchungen*. XXXIX 4, Leipzig, 1913.

_____, *The Praktikos & Chapters on Prayer*, PG 79, 1165–1200, trans. J. E. Bamberger (Kalamazoo, Michigan: Cistercian Publications, 1972).

_____, *Sentences for Monks*. Edition H. Gressmann, *Texte und Untersuchungen*, XXXIX 4, Leipzig, 1913.

_____, *Treatise on Various Evil Thoughts*. PG 79, 1145–1164.

Evagrius the Scholastic, *Ecclesiastical History*. Edition of J. Bidez-L. Parmentier, London, 1898.

Gregory of Nazianzus, *Discourse XXXIX*. Critical text by C. Moreschini, French trans. P. Gallay, 'Sources chrétiennes', no. 358, Paris, 1990, pp 150–197.

————, *Discourse XLV*. PG 36, 624-664. French trans. E. Devolder in *Saint Grégoire de Nazianze*, 'Les Écrits des saints', Namur, 1962, pp 118–162.

————, *Funeral Oration on the Great Basil (Discourse* XLIII). Vol. VII, Nicene and Post-Nicene Fathers, series II, P. Schaff (ed.) (New York: Christian Literature Publishing Co., 1893).

————, *Moral Poems*. PG 37, 521–968.

Gregory of Nyssa, *On the Making of Man*. PG 44, 128–256.*On the Soul and the Resurrection*, PG 46, 12–160. *On Virginity*. Vol. V, Nicene and Post-Nicene Fathers, series II, P. Schaff (ed.), (New York: Christian Literature Publishing Co., 1892).

————, Homily 3 *On Pascha and the Resurrection*, PG 46, 652–681.

Gregory the Great, *Life of Saint Benedict*. PL 66, 125–204. English trans. 'P. W.' and printed at Paris in 1608. Re-edited by Edmund G. Gardner in 1911.

————, *Moralia on Job*. PL 75–76.

Gregory Palamas, *To the Most Reverend Nun Xenia*. PG 150, 1044–1088. Trans. G. E. H. Palmer, P. Sherrard, K. Ware, in *The Philokalia*, vol. 4 (London/Boston: Faber and Faber, 1995), pp 293–322.

————, *Topics of Natural and Theological Science and on the Moral and Ascetic life*, trans. G. E. H. Palmer, P. Sherrard, K. Ware, in *The Philokalia*, vol. 4, (London/Boston: Faber and Faber, 1995), pp 346–417.

————, *Prosopopoeia*. PG 150, 1347–1372.

————, *Triades pour la défense des saints hésychastes*. Critical text and French trans. by J. Meyendorff, 2 vols., Louvain, 1973. Partial English trans. N. Gendle, *Gregory Palamas, The Triads* (Mahwah, New Jersey, 1983).

Hermas, *The Shepherd*. Eng. trans. in *Ante-Nicene Fathers*, vol. 2, A. Roberts and J. Donaldson (ed.), American edition, 1886.

Hesychios the Priest, *On Watchfulness and Holiness,* trans. G. E. H. Palmer, P. Sherrard, K. Ware, in *The Philokalia*, vol. 1 (London/Boston: Faber and Faber, 1979), pp 162–198.

Histoire des moines d'Égypte. Text edited by A.-J. Festugière in 'Subsidia Hagiographica', no. 34, 1961. French trans. by A.-J. Festugière, *Les Moines d'Orient*, VI/1, *Enquête sur les moines d'Égypte*, Paris, 1964.

Ignatius of Antioch, *To the Philadelphians*. Eng. trans. in *Ante-Nicene Fathers*, vol. 1, A. Roberts and J. Donaldson (ed.), American edition, 1886.

Irenaeus, *Against the Heresies*. Eng. trans. in *Ante-Nicene Fathers*, vol. 1, A. Roberts and J. Donaldson (ed.), American edition, 1886.

Isaac the Syrian, *Ascetical Homilies*. Text of the Greek version edited by Nicephore Theotoki, Leipzig, 1770, re-edited by J. Spetsieris, Athens, 1895. Eng. trans.(Boston, MA: Holy Transfiguration Monastery, 1984).

―――, *Letters.*French trans. by J. Touraille in Isaac le Syrien, *Œuvres spirituelles*, Paris, 1981, pp356–395 and 451–496.

Jean le Solitaire, *Dialogue sur l'âme et les passions des hommes*. French trans. from Syriac based on the edition of S. Dedering by I. Hausherr, Rome, 1939.

Jean Rufus, *Plérophories*. Édition F. Nau, Patrologia Orientalis, t. VIII, pp178–179.

John Cassian, *The Conferences*, trans. B. Ramsey (New York: Newman Press: 1997).

―――, *The Institutes*, trans. B. Ramsey (New York: Newman Press, 200).

John Chrysostom, *Œuvres complètes*. PG 47–64. Translation under the direction of M. Jeannin, 11 vols., Bar-le-Duc, 1863–1867.

John Climacus, *The Ladder of Divine Ascent*. Text established by Sophronios the Hermit, Constantinople, 1883, new ed. Athens, 1979. Trans. C. Luibheid and N. Russell (New York: Paulist Press, 1982) and trans. L. Moore et al. (Boston, MA: Holy Transfiguration Monastery, 1978).

John of Damascus, *The Orthodox Faith*. PG 94, 789–1228. Trans. F. H. Chase, Jr. (Washington, DC: Catholic University of America Press, 1958).

―――, *On the Virtues and the Vices*. PG 95, 85–97. Trans. G.E.H. Palmer, P. Sherrard, K. Ware in *The Philokalia*, vol. 2 (London/Boston: Faber and Faber, 1981), pp334–342.

John of Amida (of Ephesus), *Lives of the Eastern Saints*. Syriac text edited with translation by E. W. Brooks, *Patrologia Orientalis*, t. XIX, 1926.

John of Gaza, *Letters*. Edition of Nicodemos of the Holy Mountain, Venice, 1816, reprinted by S. N. Schoinas, Volos, 1960. French trans. L. Regnault, P. Lernaire, and B. Outtier in Barsanuphe et Jean, *Correspondance*, Solesmes, 1972.

John Moschus, *The Spiritual Meadow,*. PG 87, 2851–3116. Trans. J. Wortley (Kalamazoo, MI: Cistercian Publications, 1992).

Justin, *Apologies* 1 and 2. Eng. trans. in *Ante-Nicene Fathers*, vol. 1, A. Roberts and J. Donaldson (ed.), American edition, 1886.

———, *On the Resurrection*. Eng. trans. in *Ante-Nicene Fathers*, vol. 1, A. Roberts and J. Donaldson (ed.), American edition, 1886.

Léontios de Néapolis, *Vie de Syméon le Fou et Vie de Jean de Chypre*. Text established by L. Rydén and A.-J. Festugière, French translation and commentary by A.-J. Festugière, Paris, 1974. Partial Eng. trans. Derek Krueger, *Symeon the holy fool: Leontius's Life and the late antique city*, (Berkeley: University of California Press, 1996).

Makarios, *St Symeon Metaphrastis: Paraphrase of the Homilies of St Makarios of Egypt*, trans. G.E.H. Palmer, P. Sherrard, K. Ware, in *The Philo-kalia*, vol. 3 (London/Boston: Faber and Faber, 1984), pp 285–353.

Mark the Ascetic, *On Those who Think that They are Made Righteous by Works*. PG 65, 929–965. Trans. G.E.H. Palmer, P. Sherrard, K. Ware, in *The Philokalia*, vol. 1 (London/Boston: Faber and Faber, 1979), pp 125–146.

———, *On Baptism*. PG 65, 985A–1028C. French trans. C.-A. Zirnheld in Marc le moine, *Traités spirituels et théologiques*, 'Spiritualité orientale', no. 41, Bellefontaine, 1985, pp 91–121.

Maximus the Confessor, *Ad Thalassium*. PG 90, 244–785. French trans. E. Ponsoye, *Questions à Thalassios* Paris, 1992. Partial Eng. trans. in *On the Cosmic Mystery of Jesus Christ. Selected Writings from St Maximus the Confessor*, trans. P.M. Blowers and R.L. Wilken (Crestwood, NY: St Vladimir's Seminary Press, 2003).

———, *Ambigua*. PG 91, 1032–1417. French trans. E. Ponsoye, Saint Maxime le Confesseur, *Ambigua—Apories*, Nîmes, 1989. Partial Eng. trans. in *On the Cosmic Mystery of Jesus Christ. Selected Writings from St Maximus the Confessor*, trans. P.M. Blowers and R.L. Wilken (Crestwood, NY: St Vladimir's Seminary Press, 2003).

———, *Centuries on Charity*. PG 90, 960-1080, trans. G.E.H. Palmer, P. Sherrard, K. Ware, in *The Philokalia*, vol. 2 (London/Boston: Faber and Faber, 1981), pp 53–113. Also consulted: *Maximus Confessor, Selected Writings* (New York/Mahwah/Toronto: Paulist Press, 1985), pp 35–87.

———, *The Church's Mystagogy*. PG 91, 657–718. Trans. G.C. Berthold, in *Maximus Confessor, Selected Writings* (New York/Mahwah/Toronto: Paulist Press, 1985), pp 183–214.

———, *Letters*. PG 91, 364–669. French trans. E. Ponsoye, Saint Maxime le Confesseur, *Correspondance*, Nîmes, 1988.

———, *Theological and Polemical Opuscules*. PG 91, 9–285. French trans. E. Ponsoye, Saint Maxime le Confesseur, *Opuscules théologique et polemiques* (Paris: Cerf, 1998).

Methodius of Olympus, *The Banquet*. Eng. trans. in *Ante-Nicene Fathers*, vol. 6, A. Roberts and J. Donaldson (ed.), American edition, 1886.

Nemesius of Emesa, *Of the Nature of Man*. PG 40, 504–818. Trans. and ed. W. Telfer (Philadelphia: Westminster Press, 1955).

Nicetas Stethatos, *Centuries*. Trans. G. E. H. Palmer, P. Sherrard, K. Ware, in *The Philokalia*, vol. 4 (London/Boston: Faber and Faber, 1995), pp79–174.

———, *On the Soul*. Critical text and French trans. J. Darrouzès in Nicétas Stéthatos, *Opuscules et lettres*, 'Sources chrétiennes', no. 81, Paris, 1961, pp56–153.

———, *Letters*. Ibid., pp228–291.

———, *Life of Symeon the New Theologian*. Greek text and French trans. I. Hausherr, 'Orientalia christiana', no. 12, Rome, 1928.

Origen, *Against Celsus*. Eng. trans. in *Ante-Nicene Fathers*, vol. 4, A. Roberts and J. Donaldson (ed.), American edition, 1886.

Palladius, *Dialogue sur la vie de Jean Chrysostome*. Critical text and trans. A.-M. Malingrey, 'Sources chrétiennes', 341 and 342, Paris, 1988.

———, *Lausaic History*. Trans. W. K. L. Clarke (London: SPCK, and NY: Macmillan, both 1918).

Philotheos of Sinai, *Forty Texts on Watchfulness*, trans. G. E. H. Palmer, P. Sherrard, K. Ware, in *The Philokalia*, vol. 3 (London/Boston: Faber and Faber, 1984), pp16–31.

Symeon the New Theologian, *The Practical and Theological Chapters and the Three Theological Discourses*. Critical text and French trans. by J. Darrouzès, 'Sources chrétiennes', 51 and 122, Paris, 1957 and 1966. Eng. trans. P. McGuckin (Kalamazoo, MI: Cistercian Publications, 1982).

Tertullian, *Treatise on the Soul*. Édition J. H. Waszink, Q. S. F. *Tertulliani De Anima*, Amsterdam, 1947. Eng. trans. in *Ante-Nicene Fathers*, vol. 3, A. Roberts and J. Donaldson (ed.), American edition, 1886.

Thalassios the Libyan, *Centuries on Love, Self-control, and Life in accordance with the Intellect*. PG 91, 1427–1470. Trans. G. E. H. Palmer, P. Sherrard, K. Ware, in *The Philokalia*, vol. 1 (London/Boston: Faber and Faber, 1979), pp307–332.

Theodore of Petra, *Life of St Theodosius.* Text estab. by H. Usener, *Der heilige Theodosios, Schriften des Theodoros und Kyrillos*, Leipzig, 1890. French trans. A.-J. Festugière, *Les Moines d'Orient*, III/3, Paris, 1961.

Theodoret of Cyrus, *On Divine Providence.* PG 83, 555–774. Trans. T. Halton (New York: Newman Press, 1988).

Theodoret of Cyrus. *A History of the Monks of Syria.* Critical text and French trans. P. Canivet and A. Leroy-Molinghen, 'Sources chrétiennes', 234 and 257, Paris, 1977 and 1979. Eng. trans. R. M. Price (Kalamazoo, MI: Cistercian Publications, 1985).

———, *Thérapeutique des maladies helléniques.* Critical text and trans. P. Canivet, 'Sources chrétiennes', no. 57, Paris, 1958.

LIVES

Andrew Salos. PG 111, 628C-888D.

Anthony. PG 26, 835–976. *Athanasius: Selected Writings and Letters*, vol. IV, *Nicene and Post-Nicene Fathers*, series II, P. Schaff (ed.) (New York: Christian Literature Publishing Co., 1892).

Athanase l'Athonite. Text established by L. Petit, *Analecta Bollandiana*, 25, 1906, pp 5–89. French trans. D. O. R., Chevetogne, 1963.

Cyrille le Philéote. Edition and trans. E. Sargologos, 'Subsidia hagiographica', no. 39, Bruxelles, 1964.

Daniel le Scétiote. Edition of the Greek text by L. Clugnet, *Revue de l'Orient chrétien*, 5, 1900, chap. III, pp 60–62.

Jean de Chypre. Text, trans. and commentary by A.-J. Festugière in *Léontios de Néapolis, Vie de Syméon le Fou et Vie de Jean de Chypre*, Paris, 1974, pp 257–632.

Marc le Fou. Chapter III of *Vie et récits de l'abbé Daniel le Scétiote*, L. Clugnet (ed.), *Revue de l'Orient chrétien*, 5, 1900, pp 60–62.

Maxime le Kausokalybite. F. Haïkin, 'Deux vies de S. Maxime le Kausokalybite, ermite au mont Athos, XIVᵉ siècle', *Analecta Bollandiana*, 54, 1936, pp 38–112.

Priscus. Syriac text edited with translation by E. W. Brooks in John of Amida, *Lives of the Eastern Saints*, Patrologia Orientalis, t. XIX, 1926, pp 179-185.

Sabbas the Younger. Edition Papadopoulos-Kerameus, *Analekta Ierosolumitikes Stakhuologias*, V, Saint Petersburg, 1898, pp 190–359.

Symeon the Fool. Derek Krueger, *Symeon the holy fool: Leontius's Life and the late antique city* (Berkeley: University of California Press, 1996), pp 131–171.

Syméon le Nouveau Théologien. Life by Nicetas Stethatos. Greek text and French trans. I. Hausherr, 'Orientalia christiana', no. 12, Rome, 1928.

Theodore of Sykeon. Life in *Three Byzantine Saints: Contemporary Biographies of St. Daniel the Stylite, St. Theodore of Sykeon and St. John the Almsgiver*, trans. Elizabeth Dawes (London: 1948).

Theophilus and Maria. Syriac text edited with translation by E. W. Brooks in John of Amida, *Lives of the Eastern Saints*, Patrologia Orientalis, t. XIX, 1926, pp 164–179.

STUDIES

Adnès (A.) and Canivet (P.), 'Guérisons miraculeuses et exorcismes dans *l'Histoire philothée* de Théodoret de Cyr', *Revue de l'histoire des religions*, 171, 1967, pp 166–174.

Alexander (F. G.) and Selesnick (S. T.), *Histoire de la psychiatrie*, Paris, 1972.

Amundsen (D. W.) and Ferngren (G. B.), 'Medicine and Religion: Early Christianity Through the Middle Ages', in M. E. Marty and K. L. Vaux (eds.), *Health/Medicine and the Faith Traditions*, Philadelphia, 1982.

Alliez (J.) et Huber (J.-P.), 'L'Acédie ou le déprimé entre le péché et la maladie', *Annales médico-psychologiques*, 145, 1987, pp 393–407.

Arbesman (R.), '*The Daemonium Meridianum* in Greek and Latin Exegesis', *Traditio*, 14, 1958, pp 17–31.

Bardy (G.), 'Acédie', *Dictionnaire de spiritualité*, t. I, Paris, 1937, col. 166-169.

Benz (E.), 'Heilige Narrheit', *Kyrios*, 3, 1938, pp 1–55.

Böcher (O.), *Christus Exorcista. Dämonismus und Taufe im Neuen Testament*, Stuttgart, 1972.

Brunet (F.), 'Les Médecins grecs depuis la mort de Galien jusqu'à la fin de l'empire d'Orient', in Laignel-Lavastine, *Histoire générale de la médecine*, Paris, 1936, t. I, pp 433–463.

Bunge (G.), *Akèdia. La doctrine spirituelle d'Évagre le Pontique sur l'acédie*, 'Spiritualité orientale', no. 52, Bellefontaine, 1991.

Canivet (P.), 'Erreurs de spiritualité et troubles psychiques. À propos d'un passage de la vie de S. Théodose par Théodore de Pétra (530)', *Recherches de science religieuse*, 50, 1962, pp 161–205.

————, *Le Monachisme syrien selon Théodoret de Cyr*, Paris 1977.

————, see Adnès (A.) and Canivet (P.)

Chrysostomos (Bishop), 'Demonology in the Orthodox Church: A Psychological Perspective', *The Greek Orthodox Theological Review*, 33, 1988, pp 45–61.

Congourdeau (M.-H.), 'L'Animation de l'embryon humain chez Maxime le Confesseur', *Nouvelle revue théologique*, 111, 1989, pp 693–709.

Dols (M.), 'Insanity in Byzantine and Islamic Medicine', in J. Scarborough (ed.). *Symposium on Byzantine Medicine*, Dumbarton Oaks Papers, 38, 1984, pp 135–148.

Driscoll (J.), 'Listlessness in the "Mirror of Monks"', *Cistercian Studies*, 24, 1989, pp 206–214.

Ey (H.), *Études psychiatriques*, I and III, Paris, 1952 and 1954.

————, 'Histoire de la psychiatrie', *Encyclopédie médico-chirurgicale*, 1955, 37005 A.

Ey (H.), Bernard (P.), Brisset (C.), *Manuel de psychiatrie*, Paris, 1974 (4ᵉ édition).

Festugière (A.-J.), *L'Idéal religieux des Grecs et l'Évangile*, Paris, 1932.

————, *Les Moines d'Orient*, 1. Culture ou sainteté, Paris, 1961.

————, Introduction and commentary for Léontios de Néapolis, *Vie de Syméon le Fou et Vie de Jean de Chypre*, Paris, 1974.

————, 'Étude sur la Vie de S. Sabas le Jeune qui simulait la folie', in Léontios de Néapolis, *Vie de Syméon le Fou et Vie de Jean de Chypre*, Paris, 1974, pp 223–249.

Flashar (H.), *Melancholie und Melancholiker in den medizinischen Theorien der Antike*, Berlin, 1966.

Foucault (M.), *Histoire de la folie à l'âge classique*, Paris, 1972.

Fox (M.M.), The Life and Times of St. Basil the Great as Revealed in his Works, 'Catholic University Patristic Séries', no. 57, Washington, 1939, pp 13–17.

Goraïnoff (I.), *Les Fols en Christ*, Paris, 1983.

Goritcheva (T.), 'Cynisme, folie en Christ et sainteté', *Contacts*, 134, 1986, pp 90–107.

Grosdidier de Matons (J.), 'Les Thèmes d'édification dans la Vie d'André Salos', *Travaux et mémoires du Centre de recherche d'histoire et de civilisation byzantines*, IV, Paris, 1970, pp 77–328.

Guillaumont (A.), *Les 'Kephalaia gnostica' d'Evagre le Pontique et l'histoire de l'origénisme chez les Grecs et les Syriens*, Paris, 1962.

———, 'Le dépaysement comme forme d'ascèse dans le monachisme ancien', Ecole pratique des hautes études, V^e section. Sciences religieuses. *Annuaire 1968-1969*, t. LXXVI, Paris, 1968, pp 31–58, reprinted in A. Guillaumont, *Aux origines du monachisme chrétien*, Bellefontaine, 1979, pp 89–116.

———, 'Le Travail manuel dans le monachisme ancien. Contestation et valorisation', *Troisième Colloque d'histoire des religions organisé par la Société Ernest Renan, Société française d'histoire des religions*, 1978, Orsay 1979, pp 31–58, reprinted in A. Guillaumont, *Aux origines du monachisme chrétien*, Bellefontaine, 1979, pp 117–126.

Guillaumont (A. and C.), Introduction to Évagre le Pontique, *Traité pratique*, 'Sources chrétiennes', no. 170, Paris, 1971, pp 84–90.

Jackson (S. W.), 'Galen—On Mental Disorders', *Journal of the History of Behavioural Science*, 5, 1969, pp 365–384.

Keenan (A.M.), 'St. Gregory of Nazianzus and Early Byzantine Medicine', *Bulletin of the History of Medicine*, 9, 1941, pp 8–30.

———, 'St Gregory of Nyssa and the Medical Profession', *Bulletin of the History of Medicine*, 15, 1944, pp 150–161.

Kovalevsky (I.), *Jurodstvo o Xriste i Xrista radi jurodivye*, Moscou, 1900.

Larchet (J.-C.), *Thérapeutique des maladies spirituelles* (Paris: Éditions de l'Ancre, 1991).

———, *Théologie de la maladie*, (Paris: Cerf, 1991). Eng. trans. J. & M. Breck, *The Theology of Illness* (Crestwood, NY: St Vladimir's Seminary Press, 2002).

Lecomte (B.), *L'Acédie: invention et devenir d'une psychopathologie dans le monde monastique*, doctoral thesis in medicine, Université de Nancy, 1991.

Lossky (V.), *Mystical Theology of the Eastern Church*, trans. members of the Fellowship of St Alban and St Sergius (Crestwood, NY: St Vladimir's Seminary Press, 1997).

Louf (A.), 'L'Acédie chez Évagre le Pontique', *Concilium*, 99, 1974, pp 113–117.

Meyendorff (J.), *Byzantine Theology*, 2d ed. (New York: Fordham University Press, 1979).

———, *Le Christ dans la théologie byzantine* (Paris: Cerf, 1969).

Miller (T.S.), *The Birth of the Hospital in the Byzantine Empire*, Baltimore, 1985.

Nutton (V.), 'From Galen to Alexander, Aspects of Medicine and Medieval Practice in Late Antiquity', in J. Scarborough (ed.). *Symposium on Byzantine Medicine*, Dumbarton Oaks Papers, 38, 1984, pp 1–14.

Pélicier (Y.), *Histoire de la psychiatrie*, Paris, 1971.

Petzold (H.), 'Zur Frömmigkeit der heiligen Narren', in *Die Einheit der Kirche, Festgabe P. Meinhold*, Wiesbaden, 1977, pp 140–153.

Roccatagliata (G.), *Storia della psichiatria antica*, Milan, 1973.

Ryden (L.), 'The Holy Fool', in S. Hackel (ed.). *The Byzantine Saint*, 'Studies Supplementary to Sobornost', no. 5, London, 1981, pp 106–113.

Saward (J.), *Perfect Fools: Folly for Christ's Sake in Catholic and Orthodox Spirituality* (New York: Oxford University Press, 1980).

Sémelaigne (A.), *Études historiques sur l'aliénation mentale dans l'Antiquité*, Paris, 1869.

Sendrail (M.), *Histoire culturelle de la maladie*, Toulouse, 1980.

Sophrony (Archimandrite), 'Des fondements de l'ascèse orthodoxe', *Messager de l'exarchat du Patriarche russe en Europe occidentale*, 17, 1954, pp 30–42.

Spanneut (M.), *Le Stoïcisme des Pères de l'Église de Clément de Rome à Clément d'Alexandrie*, Paris, 1957.

Spidlik (T.), '"Fous pour le Christ" en Orient', *Dictionnaire de spiritualité*, v, 1964, col. 752–758.

Stéphanou (E.), 'La Coexistence initiale de l'âme et du corps d'après saint Grégoire de Nysse et Maxime l'Homologète', *Échos d'Orient*, 31, 1932, pp 304–315.

Syrkin (A.Y.), 'On the Behavior of the "Fools for Christ's Sake"', *History of Religions*, 22, 1982, pp 150–171.

Milton Keynes UK
Ingram Content Group UK Ltd.
UKHW011547050624
443786UK00023B/92